intimate moments

A Collection of Haibun

intimate moments

A Collection of Haibun

Gary R. Ford

intimate moments

Published by Insight Publishers
Address: Thorsby, Alberta, Canada
Website: http://garyrford.ca/insight

Edited, designed and typeset by the Author
Cover Image Photo by Aryn Ford
Fonts: Hanzipen SC, Times New Roman
Software: MS Word, OpenOffice TextWriter, Adobe Acrobat Pro,
Illustrator, Photoshop, Lightroom, CreateSpace

ISBN: 978-0-9939737-3-4
Printed in the United States of America or Canada
10 9 8 7 6 5 4 3 2 1

DEDICATION

Dedicated to members of my family, and those friends that have been stimulants for my writing, sometimes appearing in haibun form, possibly with names changed to disguise the innocent.

Table of Contents

Introduction

Intimate Moments

Intimate moments are the private, closely personal, intimate affairs of life. Although intimate affairs can be deep, dark, significant, closely held secrets, they can also be plain moments of awareness of mundane and everyday issues.

Intimate moments may involve a physical connection with others – eye contact, a simple touch, a hug, sexual contact; but also occur through conversation, a sharing of private thoughts, feelings, awareness, and memories. Sharing the emotional responses we have to our environment and the people we're with, our interpretations of events and our thoughts about them is a form of deep intimacy.

In this collection of haibun, I endeavor to share intimate moments and something of myself with you the reader. These moments are not generally tumultuous. They are just some of the simple moments in a life. For various reasons, I found them to be significant enough to write about them. I offer each haibun to you for your reading pleasure and hopefully to stimulate your own reflections on similarly important intimate moments in your own life.

Intentions

Writing haibun over the past ten years, there have been many intimate moments finding their way onto the screen of my computer. It seems the origins of my haibun reside in either memories; my awareness of a here and now moment; my feelings about certain things like aging, relationships, grief; or, a reaction to something I read or hear.

I offer these different moments as an intimate gesture to you, the reader. I offer to you what I crave myself. I so desire moments when I can sit with another person and hear his or her stories, come to an understanding of how this person thinks, feels, apprehends his or her world. In such sharing, I'm drawn closer to the person and to myself through identification and comparison. I have another looking glass with which to look back on myself and compare the other person's experiences with my own.

I hope what you read here enhances your own reflection on self, maybe even brings you some new "ah ha" moments, and in some way, even if just briefly, reduces your loneliness. I assume that like me, you experience how alone we each are in how we uniquely encounter our world. At the nub of it all, we come into this life, travel through it, and depart in our own way. You may be able to increase your awareness of your way by comparing it with mine.

A single haibun can easily be read in one short sitting. Ideally, you can read one of my moments, set the book down, and reflect on something of your own that might be triggered by what I've written. Perhaps you can look for yourself as you reflect on my moment. In such looking, new insights might emerge and enrich your own sense of self.

I envision you reading these haibun while sitting like Rodin's "Thinker" on your own personal throne; or reading as you stand in the kitchen waiting for a pot of water to come to a boil; or reading while traveling to work on the bus or train; or grabbing the book as you crawl into bed to read just one haibun to stimulate your own subconscious mind during sleep. Wherever you read this, I hope I touch you in some way.

If I'm lucky, I will have stimulated you to take the opportunity to write your own haibun. Put pen to paper, or finger to keyboard, and allow your own words to surface as you share your own intimate moments with page or screen. Then share what you write with others, either through notes to friends, publication or posting on the web – let others benefit from your own intimate moments.

Why Haibun?

For several reasons, I have chosen to write in the haibun style. Haibun tend to occupy a page or less, and work well to show a brief memory, a single moment of awareness, a quick reaction to something in one's environment.

The style is poetic when done well, and as an old fart, writing haibun gives me an opportunity to stretch long-dormant poetic muscles. I get to reach for words and phrases that show versus tell, and I find pleasure when something seems to emerge from unconscious processes to appear in my writing.

Sitting down to write a haibun is a singular event. I don't have to start from the last piece of writing and continue on to the next. I just need to capture the brief moment on which I'm focussed when sitting at my computer. Overtime, themes do appear and this book has been organized according to those themes, but the act of writing can be quite random.

There is a meditative quality to conceiving and writing down a haibun, and particularly when composing the haiku that are associated with haibun prose. The pace is both Zen-like and deliberate – rhythmic movement of fingers as the words come to mind along with frequent pauses as the reflection takes place. There is also a form of life review in the search for haibun content. It is relaxing and satisfying to dredge up memories, to recall moments of here-and-now awareness, to reflect on the human condition, foibles and all.

If you are already familiar with the haibun writing style, you might want to skip to page 12 to begin reading the first section of haibun. Otherwise, if you are new to haibun, I offer below my own answers to the question, "What is haibun?"

What is Haibun?

Haibun is a genre of writing, sometimes considered a variant of poetry, in which the overall style is intended to be haiku like:

- descriptive (showing versus telling),

- brief (words are chosen carefully and there is no rigid adherence to the rules of grammar),

- natural (references to natural phenomenon),

- possessing a whole meaning greater than the sum of the parts.

Haibun began in Japan during the 1600s and the first examples of this form of prose poetry are attributed to the famous haiku poet, Matsuo Basho – a traveling monk who initially gained great fame for his haiku works. He periodically escaped from the adulation of his fans and travelled on foot many miles in the Japanese wilderness visiting ancient religious sites. During these journeys, he kept travel journals comprised of descriptions of the places he visited interspersed with self reflections in prose and haiku.

Basho shared much of his own awareness, reflections, and humour in this form, gaining more fame for his creative writing. This writing was emulated by his students and continued over time. More recently, haibun gained use by writers in the English language. Publications such as A Hundred Gourds, Bottle Rockets, Contemporary Haibun and Contemporary Haibun Online, Frog Pond, Haibun Today, Modern Haiku, Notes from the Gean, Simply Haiku and The Heron's Nest have all featured haibun and haiku.

Haibun Elements

Discussions continue as to what makes a good haibun, especially when written in the English language. To be different from other forms of poetic writing and specifically be seen as haibun, a piece would generally satisfy the following expectations:

- contain prose and one or more haiku, senryu or tanka,

- be written predominantly in the present tense,

- follow the haiku principles of brevity, brief descriptive phrases, and sentence fragments,

- be rooted in nature or natural human experience,

- on one hand, the writer is to be a detached observer of natural phenomena, and

- on the other hand, the observation of something else links back to the writer through some form of epiphany or expanded self-awareness.

For example, I wrote this haibun after selling out of the business I had started and operated for twenty years:

Spider's Bounty

Time on my hands and with no business to attend to, I watch others work at theirs while I contemplate my relationship with the former business partner that took over the business.

Outside my window, a wolf spider sits in the center of his evening's work – a web glistening with drops of dew, swaying in a slight breeze. Perched over a silk sarcophagus, the spider sucks on the juices of a fat blue bottle fly.

Did the fly sense the end coming? Did I?

> an ebony pen
> on the page
> empty

This example includes a title, prose and haiku, shows brevity and descriptive phrasing, contains reference to nature, is written predominantly in the present tense, and the author is both the detached observer and present in the conclusion.

The Title

In effective haibun, the title is a significant aspect of a piece. The title can simply lead the reader into the prose. It can also add to the greater meaning by acting in relationship to both the prose and haiku, senryu or tanka contained within the haibun. A well-selected title can extend the artistry of a piece.

The Prose

A good haibun stirs emotion, even if just pleasure in the choice of words and images described. It has an aesthetic appeal in that it describes something that triggers one or more of the senses – sight, sound, smell, taste, touch, – enough to produce a visceral reaction – either one of pleasure, pain, or churn. This might be accomplished through pure description using well-selected descriptive language or through the use of metaphor or simile relating to other parallel experiences.

A good haibun has elements of poetry within the prose – words with power as they describe, rhythm in the singsong of phrases, and images that crystallize in the mind. Words with power are action words, words with leverage in their description so that the thing being described seems more present, more alive. If past tense is used, the words bring the described experience alive as if it is happening now.

The words, the sentences, even the paragraphs are structured to move the reader further and further into the moment. The rhythm matches the experience being described – fast and urgent if tension is involved, slow and melancholy if one of deeper reflection, languorous if one of seduction.

For me, a strong haibun is one that relates to basic aspects of being human, or triggers us to think about these basic and universal elements:

- birth, life and death including any specific stages of development from birth to death;

- relationships between living beings including general companionship, family, intimate friends, moments of bonding, sex, conflict, dissolution of relationships, and discovery about oneself through relationship;

- trials and tribulations that challenge us to be better than we are, whether we succeed or fail;

- general values that are part of what it means to be human;

- spiritual matters that involve exploration of questions about life's purpose, our place in the universe, our relationship to something beyond ourselves; and,

- our foibles and limitations that can be examined with a humorous eye.

I think the power of any haibun is in its ability to move the widest body of readers, or to deeply move a targeted audience. If this is the measure, then there is tremendous freedom of style within the form.

Haiku

A haibun is prose mixed with one or more haiku. Haiku is the most widely practiced poetry form in the world. Based on speech sounds in Japan, the tradition of haiku in Japan required a 5-7-5 syllable poem. However Japanese is very different in speech sounds when compared to spoken English. As a result, English language haiku do not generally follow that tradition.

Typically twelve to thirteen syllables in English would correlate to the seventeen syllables in the Japanese language. For this reason, concern about syllable count has not become a strong tradition in English language haiku writing. There is much more acceptance of haiku regardless of the number of syllables. English language haiku are generally faithful to the other traditions of brevity, description, two fragments juxtaposed to each other, and the reach for a meaning larger than the parts.

In the original tradition of haiku, the three lines were descriptive of nature. For example, in a classic haiku written by Basho and translated into English by Allen Ginsberg,

> the old pond,
> a frog jumped in:
> kerplunk!

These brief three lines describe an observed moment in nature and give us a humorous look at both frog and Basho's appreciation of and amusement with the moment. Perhaps, Basho saw himself in the frog, seeing his own life as a mere "kerplunk" in the span of time.

When looking at haiku in the haibun genre, the following expectations generally prevail:

- the haiku should be a true haiku in the Japanese tradition, generally comprised of two fragments, typically composed with two lines and a juxtaposing third,

- the haiku should not restate the prose but should extend it through contrast, juxtaposition, offering something just beyond the prose,

- the haiku should be comprised of descriptions of natural phenomenon, or be a senryu which contains humorous descriptions of the human condition, and

- the reader should experience a bit of an "ah ha" moment in comprehension of a meaning larger than the two separate fragments within the haiku.

Some proponents of the haibun genre emphasize haiku should be able to stand alone. It's great when this happens, but I think the prose gives context to most haiku used in haibun just as the haiku gives something extra to the prose, and that relationship is most satisfying for me.

Senryu

Very much a haiku form, senryu are much more about human experience, emotion, or nature. Senryu often have a humorous quality to them as they show something of the foibles of being human. As an example of senryu showing us something of the human condition, Carol Raisfeld wrote and posted the following on her website haikubuds.com (*cited with permission*):

> bird by bird
> the toddler kisses
> her story book

This three-line poem conveys something universal. We can envision a young child, feeling the specialness of her book and the images within. She conveys that appreciation through the loving act of kissing the images. This reminds us of how, as adults, we can be childlike in how we hold possessions as precious and protect our own property from others. It also shows us something about how deeply, innocently, and completely we can love.

Tanka

An extension of haiku, tanka takes the form of five lines, often comprised of a fragment of three lines and a juxtaposing fragment of two lines. For example, Chen-ou Liu, wrote the following tanka published in Haibun Today in December 2009 (*cited with permission*):

> birthday cakes
> one on top
> of another
> pushing me down
> six feet under

The first three lines give us information about a context and the last two lines give us information about how this image impacts the author. Tanka, like haiku, can stand on their own bringing an "ah ha" moment to the reader, or can work with and extend the prose in a haibun, adding to the fuller meaning of a piece.

Summary

Haibun, considered a form of prose poetry, are the ideal vehicle for sharing brief intimate moments in written form. The combination of title, prose, and haiku, senryu or tanka add deeper meaning to the written words. The form is meditative in nature and writing of haibun is very conducive to self-reflection.

Memories

The content of each of these haibun was stimulated by a particular memory. Most often they are a description of a moment in my childhood past, but some are from events later in life to which I attributed some significance.

Gopher Holes

Flat prairie land – endless, stubbled, punctuated by small hills created by nearby gophers. Heads bob at burrow entrances. Regular peeps advise neighbors they aren't alone, while shrill whistles warn of danger.

In the distance, a Red Tail rides the thermals and silently glides overhead.

My companions and I, seven years old, dig our underground fort. This morning, to get an early start, we left our homes without telling a soul. We find adventure in secrecy. Confident that no one knows about our hideout, we speak in fantasies as we cut deep in the earth, gouge out soil to create overhangs, drag logs over the opening to make a roof.

> the air sighs
> as the hawk dives
> my dad calls my name

Running

Now 64, I run in the deep water of an Aqua-fit course. The instruction is to run as fast as we can for 30 seconds. My full out speed lasts only a few seconds, drops off quickly.

A flash recollection – as a teenager engaged in team football drills, I was one of the quickest – for the first twenty-five yards – and then, as if suddenly weighted by an anchor, I'd slow, lose all ability to move with grace. My teammates passed me by with jeers and taunts. I hung my head.

And then a second memory surfaces: He stands in the doorway at the back of our house. Four years old, I ignored his first request to come in. His eyes have that stern look that says 'do as you're told'. I stick my tongue out, see that look suddenly change to intense anger. I launch myself down the sidewalk, circle around to the front of the house, probably a distance of no more than twenty-five yards from back step to front yard. He grabs me short of the freedom I seek, throws me to the ground, takes off his belt and lets me know he is to be obeyed.

> a newly dropped fawn
> darts, zigzags, tests his legs
> the steps of an old man

Learning A New Rule

"Hello young man. Can I help you?"

He holds out two mittened hands, displaying a collection of coins. "Mister. Is this money yours?"

"I don't think so. Where did you get it?"

"I found it buried in the snow, by the telephone pole at the head of the crescent."

"Lucky you....that looks like about a dollar fifty in change. Why did you knock on my door?"

"Mum says that it belongs to someone else and I have to find out who lost it.... and... return it to them."

"You don't sound too happy about that."

"I wanted the money.... But Mom says we can't take stuff that doesn't belong to us, and I have to go to every house in the neighborhood."

"That's twenty or so houses. Where did you start?"

"At the house closest to the telephone pole. Nobody claimed it yet... "

"That's good. My house is near the end. Maybe you'll get to keep the money?"

"Nah...some people weren't home and I have to go back tonight...."

> a child's dreams
> nickel candies
> still bchind closed glass

A Polished Stone

Old, gruff, unshaven. He stares at me with a hard look. Normally silent, he starts to talk. Startled, I worry that he's caught me staring at the scar on his neck, or watching the rhythmic movement of his hands as he plays with a small stone. Something I do every time I visit my friend's home. I can't help it.

>a pocket knife
>open on the table
>an apple core turns brown

"Kid, a stranger once saved my life with this piece of rock." He holds a stone inches away from my face.

I nod, as if I understand what he's telling me… but I don't know how a stone could save his life.

"It was April, 1916. France. Know where France is kid?"

I don't but I nod my head anyway, too nervous to speak.

"We were in the trenches, muck everywhere, shells firing over our heads, the order came. Charge, take out the Huns. Fool's orders! Suicide if you asked any of us."

I try to picture what he's telling me but nothing in my life comes close to what he's talking about. I nod to show I'm paying attention.

"Well, soldiers can't stop and debate when orders come. Just have to do it, and we did. I'm not ashamed to say that I was scared as hell. Leapt out of that ditch and ran as fast as I could. Figured it was the only way to dodge what was coming at us."

Silence as he stares into the ceiling for so long I wonder if he's finished talking to me. I nervously shift from foot to foot thinking I should leave.

>a polished stone
>momentary reflections
>bring memories to the surface

A heavy intake of breath and a long sigh. "I was just lying there, on my back, looking up at the grey sky, trying to figure out what happened. A shadow loomed overhead. I looked into his eyes – the eyes of a stranger from another corp. He cussed foul, said, 'You're hit bad. You'll bleed to death if that isn't stoppered up.' I couldn't speak, move my head or nothin." Tears slowly roll down his cheeks.

That surprises me – this tough old guy crying. I don't know what to do. But that doesn't matter because he just keeps on talking as if the words had to be said and it didn't matter who, or if, anyone was there to hear.

"Then he did it. This guy reached into the mud, grabbed this here stone, stuck it in his mouth, swirled it around to get the mud off, and with his thumb, as if in slow motion, he stuck that rock in this damn hole in my neck. He spit out the dirt, mumbled 'Good luck to you mate' then he just kept on moving, moving forward into the chaos, with bullets whizzing all around us."

I can't imagine how a rock could be stuck in his neck or how this would make a difference. I want to ask him, but he seems to be talking to himself.

"You know, it was ghost like. I just lay there... in my own pocket of silence, even as all of the noise surrounded me... waiting to die..."

Again a tear slowly slides through the hairs on his face, as he stares at me without blinking, without seeing me. "This plain old stone stopped the bleeding."

> oatmeal porridge
> in a chipped bowl
> a prayer of thanks

Displaced Magic

"We had magic before the crows came... we understood our magic. ... And when they cawed that our magic was unclean, we laughed, took a little offense, even killed a few of them and pulled their feathers for our hair... But that word, unclean, that word somehow, like an illness, like its own magic, it began to grow." *

Once a "curious, adventurous, eager, ready-to-explore-the-world, touch-everything, laugh-in-amusement, stare-at-strange-things, ponder-what-all-was-about" child, at night I slept deeply, dreamt of greatness and wonder. During the day, full of energy, I ran naked, tumbled, got up again, played in the dirt, stuck my tongue out to show disdain, took things apart, spit out foods I didn't like.

Then, like a slow poison the words, "bad boy" intruded into my consciousness.

> gravel and moss
> on his gravestone –
> just five years old

* Joseph Boyden, *The Orenda*, Hamish Hamilton – Imprint of Penguin Canada Books, Inc., 2013, p.4

Milky Tears

blocks of ice
on the ground
the clink of milk bottles

The horse was just standing there. A rope from its halter trailed down to the knot on the handle of a large round cement block. Water slowly trickled from the back of the wagon. Flies buzzed around the horse's haunches. His tail flicked, swooshed back and forth.

I tried talking to the horse, but it just looked at me with its big eye, shook its head, rattled the oats in a bag hanging off its muzzle, then turned its attention back to the crunch of chewing on grain.

The knot fascinated me. So I untied it, then tried to do it up again. I worked at that for a while till a friend came running up to me. I turned, fired off my cap pistol.

"BANG! You're dead."
men yell, reach
for the reins

No Tin Soldier

It was bound to turn out this way. On TV, my buddies and I watched a movie of paratroopers dropping into enemy territory. After, our toy soldiers learned to fly – as high as we could throw them. But that didn't have the effect we wanted.

We used thread, small patches of cloth, made chutes for them. A slight tilt just before they crashed as the chute dragged a bit of air, but not much more. We figured we needed air time – more seconds for them to fall so the chutes could really open.

We climbed onto the garage roof, threw them as high as we could. They soared, free fell, then slowed dramatically as the chute grabbed air, broke their fall. Just like the movie.

That really got us to thinking. With a bit of rooting around in a closet, we found twine, a large sheet, and a ton of fantasy. Little kid fingers tied the four corners of the cotton sheet to the thin rope. Just long enough to tie the remaining ends to a belt.

I was the first to go. How this came about, I can't figure because I'm terrified of heights. I had fool's courage. I didn't even look. I just ran the full length of the peak and leapt. The chute would work – and if it didn't, an old mattress would break my fall.

I know my form was good. I did what they taught the soldiers on TV. Slight bend of the knees, arms to my sides, heels reaching for ground.

Did you know that a collarbone makes a weird sound, right by your ear, as it breaks?

> swallows ride the sky,
> dine on the fly
> many shades of blue

Life Changing Punishments

I don't remember grade three. Recently an old school chum commented that I was in the principal's office almost every day, had classroom detention for most of them. I have this vague sense that I played the role of class clown, provoking laughter, getting their attention, having fun, avoiding boredom.

> memories stir
> trembling fingers
> hold a piece of chalk

Thousands of lines were scribbled, erased, and written again.

"I will not write and pass notes in class."

"I will not disrupt the class."

"I will stop teasing others."

My neck hurt from craning my head back, a long reach upward to write on the whole surface of the blackboard. A callus formed on my right index finger. Hundreds of lines assigned as homework, hunched over a kitchen table, scribbling away, the pain of cramped fingers. Over the year, the quality of my penmanship declined, became tighter, a scrawl. I also became much more stoic, inhibited, watchful.

I reflect on the costs.

> spring thaw
> a step on the ice
> frees the water beneath

Supposed to Know

"How do I get there?" Dad's friend asks.

Dad replies "Gary can show you. We've driven there many times." and turning to me says, " You know the way, don't you?"

A rush of pride as he gives me this rare vote of confidence.

Was that a wink? For me – or for his friend?

I give directions for the first few streets, soon realize I really don't know the way. Only 8 years old, I haven't paid attention while the adults drove. Dad's friend knows, continues the charade, prompts. I pretend, give more directions.

Now 64, how familiar this experience has been. Expectations placed, knowing less than I should, pretending my way through.

> my dog stares at me
> as I sit on the couch
> dinner time?

Tall Grass

Golden grass rises to my waist. Orange, red and black, yellow, white – these poppies praise the sun. Purple blossoms excuse tall thistle stalks. With a slight whisper, a gentle breeze moves aside the wild oats as I cross the meadow. Tall grass touches my waist. I remember another time when the grass came to my shoulders.

Valerie and I had made a deal. I don't remember how it came about. Two seven-year-old kids chatting their way through the taboos, I guess. She has only sisters, no idea what a boy looks like. She offers to show me hers if I show her mine.

We go to a nearby field where the grasses are tall, no one's around. I go down first, on my back, wriggle out of my clothing. She stands looking down on my display. Naked, I suggest it's her turn.

Harshly, "What are you looking at?" shouts her older sister. I see her peek at me through the grass. Looking at Valerie with a sly grin, "Oh, you're in trouble... I'm telling mom." She dashes homeward to convey the news. Valerie whimpers a "Sorry" and follows.

Shocked, I dress quickly, walk home with trepidation, worrying about what my parents will say. I tell my mother. She chuckles, says, "It's okay."

Later, I learn that Valerie didn't fare so well – spanked, forbidden to go outside, forever prohibited from having anything to do with me.

> a cool breeze
> arrives in the night
> the grasses part

No Lunch Today

Hot, bored, crowded into the backseat as miles roll by, I can hear the whine even before the question leaves my mouth. "Is it time for lunch yet?"

"We'll stop soon enough." barks my Dad.

Finally, he pulls over at a roadside picnic area. My mother and father lug out the food cooler and utensils, set up at a table, make a stack of sandwiches. The rest of us mill about, playing in the open spaces.

At the far end of the picnic area, we hear shouts of "Bear!" People scramble from their tables, head for their cars. Simultaneously, my parents yell, "To the car". My mother turns, hands me a plate full of sandwiches, says, "Go. Now!"

She and dad each grab a handle of the cooler, crab walk it to the car. The stack of sandwiches vibrates, bounces, as I half run, half walk to hold the plate steady. Still unsighted, the bear is an ominous presence amidst the cries of "Hurry!" and "Get your ass in the car."

Beside me, my mother stumbles. I stop, turn, reach out one hand, grab her arm, help her up – just as the pile topples. Paper plate and sandwiches float in slow motion to the ground. As I'm about to stoop to gather them up, my dad yells, "Leave it – get inside".

I fling myself at the back door of our car, throw myself in. My mother gets into the front seat, slams the door, checks to see we're all inside, rests her forehead against the side window, looks at our lunch lying on the ground.

> silence in the car
> a large black dog
> ambles from the brush

Stream Fishing

Just turned twelve with a new fishing outfit – the whole deal – rod, reel, vest, lures, net, and wicker creel. Near our camp, I set out alone to walk the creek. Cool water seeps through the seams of old running shoes and slowly rises to my ankles. Stepping further into the stream, I soak my pant legs to the knee, turn downriver, send out a thin filament of nylon tied to a torpedo float and a three foot leader with a dry fly. As it drifts, I carefully steer the line under overhanging branches at stream's edge.

The water churns, the line goes tight, and the rod tip bends in a graceful arc as the fish runs downriver. A slip of the foot jerks the rod toward the sky and a curse erupts. A choking gasp becomes a relieved sigh as the fish is still there. Seconds become minutes – a many coloured trout is taken in the net, dumped with pride and a great deal of joy into my grass lined creel.

Eager to get back to camp to tell my tale, I slosh my way upstream. Mental replays run over and over again as I relish the glory of this fisherman's trophy. As I climb over a fallen tree that straddles the stream, I lurch forward, cold soak myself to the waist. But today it doesn't matter.

Back at camp, the story is told with great embellishment, the creel slowly opened to reveal the catch.

But it's empty.

in a deep pool,
a rainbow shines
– surprise ending

What Lesson Do I Learn Today?

life savings
another penny
in the piggy bank

Attending school in another neighborhood, I'm not welcome; nor do I want to be here.

He shouts his taunt, "Come on. Fight, damn it!"

Smaller than me, a bit dim witted, I know I can take him. I don't want to hurt him or embarrass him in front of the others.

"No, not today."

One of the onlookers yells, "What… chicken?"

Now feeling embarrassed, I look at the faces of the watchers. Circling around the two of us, eager to see a fight, hopeful that he'll give me a bashing.

Faster than I anticipated, he swings. His fist crashes into the right side of my face. I'm surprised at how little I feel it… as if there was no force behind the punch, confirming my belief that this fight could be easily won.

From some place I don't understand, "I dare you to hit the other cheek." And he does. In response, I lunge at him as he steps back, a smirk on his face, and I take him down.

Suddenly, the school yard supervisor of the day, our home room teacher, steps up, grabs me by the neck of my shirt, lifts me to a stand, and also with a smirk on his face, says… "You're coming with me".

the principal's office
four sharp whacks
on each hand

After the Game

Friday night in early October, we exit the locker room, showered, combed, with colour in our cheeks, pleased about our victory on the football field. My buddy and I both played well, making significant contributions.

Our breath shows in the cool evening air. Bright stars stand out in a rich black sky and moonlight casts a shadow in the far corner of the field. The stadium has cleared. Only a few stragglers stand about.

And then we see them – two young beauties, leaning against a pillar, hands in pockets, scarves over their shoulders protecting their ears and chins from the cold.

I am drawn to the one with dark hair and hazel eyes. She has a confident manner and smiles as we cockily approach. We engage in flirtatious rituals.

> the cool night air
> running down the field
> with the scent of her

She attends the high school that our team defeated, and waits for her date. We boast and tease – she laughs and teases back. I'm tackled.

> stepping back in the pocket
> he throws a `Hail Mary' pass
> cool night

I lose all awareness of my buddy as I write down her telephone number.

Was This It?

a conversation
with my school counselor
"What is my purpose?"

Hot, muggy, sweat trickling in my eyes, I seek the air conditioning of a nearby grocery store. Little did I know that seeking my own comfort might make a difference in that of others.

As I enter the store, I notice a woman holding her young infant in front of her. Anguish on her face, distress on the child's face, I ask if she's okay, if the child is choking. She turns, her arms outstretched, hands me her child. No breathing, no sounds, colour deepening. I recognize the symptoms and gently but firmly apply the Heimlich maneuver. The child bends forward, throws up all over my shoes, wails. The mother grabs her child, disappears as I stare at the mess I've made.

Cleaned up, I move onward toward the back of the store, to the frozen foods section, notice how good the coolness feels on my skin. Then I see a woman collapse, sit on the floor, lean against one of the meat coolers, begin to vibrate. Apparently, the quick shift from hot to cold has caused a seizure.

I rush over, sit down, pull her into me, cradle her so she won't bang her head. Others gather around, watch, talk about what needs to be done to make sure she doesn't harm herself. After a few minutes, she settles, realizes where she is and what has just happened, pulls away from me, sits herself against the cooler and insists she will be alright. Embarrassed, she ignores offers of assistance and asks to be left alone.

I wander off, finish my shopping, leave the store.

> no longer a chrysalis –
> the butterfly lands
> on a blossom

A Day of Firsts

I received my acceptance to university in the mail today. To celebrate, my girlfriend and I go out for dinner and our usual end of the evening.

For months, we've finished each date in my parents old Mercury, necking and steaming up the windows. Usually, this would happen in front of her house, and the flicker of the front porch light would let us know that our date was over.

Tonight, I take the initiative, drive to a relatively secluded spot, park, turn on the radio, and hug her into me. Elvis sings, "Can't Help Falling In Love With You."

Lost in the reverie of this day, in the soft lips and warm body of her kisses, I suggest we move to the back seat. I take it as permission when she opens her door and beats me into the back. There, our kissing becomes petting. I feel like I'm about to explode with excitement. Her enthusiasm seems no less, and I slip my hands under her blouse and delight in the feel of her skin and soft breasts.

With acceleration beyond my rational thinking, our pants come down, I enter her, lose myself in the sensations of her moist flesh…

But only for the tiniest of moments. I'm so excited I realize I'm about to ejaculate. I'm rapidly overwhelmed with fear, guilt, confusion. My 17-year-old angst clicks in.

I lose all awareness of her. I worry about what we're doing, what I'm doing – without protection, without consideration for our future, with many concerns about how I'm taking advantage. I pull out in deep anguish. A clumsy apology, a "we should be getting home", silence as we drive to her place, say good night.

> my life's savings
> a list of disappointed women
> in my memory bank

Mother Carry Me *

The river she is flowing, flowing and growing
The river she is flowing, down to the sea
Mother carry me, your child I will always be
Mother carry me, down to the sea

We've travelled by van and car to paddle the white water of the Red Deer River above Sundre, Alberta. Fed from melt waters draining from the Rocky Mountains, the water is cold, beautifully blue. The river carves its path through ancient rock, with many sections of rapids and small water falls at ledges that traverse the river.

The day is sunny, the air crisp, adventure ready to be had. A group of us put our kayaks in the water, push off for a three-mile run. Relatively new to kayaking, I haven't yet mastered my Eskimo roll and I'm still quite shaky in my tight fitting boat on this fast moving water.

Before long, passing over a small ledge, I tip. A first attempt at a roll is unsuccessful. Upside down, I scramble my way out of the boat, gasp for air, flail about to keep hold of my paddle and the small rope at the kayak's bow. Other paddlers change course, head in my direction to tow me to shore.

As this drama takes place, I float downstream, cold water filling the air spaces in my wet suit. I grasp the stern rope of the nearest paddler and he works his way to riverside. As he reaches a safe eddy, the current swings me into shore. I stand, blow water, gasp and laugh. What fun!

I collect my gear, climb back into my kayak, swing back out into the current to continue the trip downstream.

Later, I'm told this scene was repeated thirteen times as we moved down river. Apparently, the cold water sucked out my body heat. I flipped more and more often, became delirious, increasingly limp, prone to drift off, not paying attention to the hazards of the river.

At journey's end, they strip off my wet suit, express alarm at my low body temperature. Several lay down next to me to warm me up, others hastily make a fire to heat some water. Hypothermia can kill.

> campfire sparks
> a tin mug
> warms the hands,
> others tell stories
> of their own adventures

* Chant written by Diana Hilledebrand-Hull. A favourite of my wife, MegAnne.

Fifties on 5

Dusk, driving on a lonely road, my thoughts drift as I listen to golden oldies playing on my satellite radio.

I feel this compulsion to jump into the radio, immerse myself right into the tunes, literally transport back to my youth...

- hiding from family affairs in a basement bedroom listening to music on my transistor radio,

- saving my coins to buy the hot new 45,

- using a special adapter to play the smaller records on an old 78 player,

- imagining cool names for the band of musicians I could organize and make famous,

- cajoling young woman to dance with me at the lakeside dance pavilion,

- meeting the first love of my life on a perfect fall night while tunes play through the open windows of a nearby car.

> a breath of steam
> follows my words
> past life

Here and Now

These haibun generally relate to a moment of awareness that I consciously experienced. I seldom write in the moment so these are also memories, but tend to be a recollection of being present in and aware of my surroundings.

Spring Awakens

Robin song introduces the morning sun. Finches make their daily visit to the feeder. Dew soaked roads sparkle in the bright light. Buds open to flower. A bee loudly announces its presence. The air has a different smell, a different feel.

> rapid tick, tuck, tick
> and a pileated laugh
> – insects wake

And yet winter's depression lingers, saps energy, depletes motivation. Many things to get done and no desire to do them. My mind ruminates on failures, disappointments, and discouraging signs.

> moving slowly
> the old dog grazes on grass
> and throws up bile

Eclipse

It's a dark and quiet night, moisture in the air but no rain clouds in the sky. My dog slowly walks along, stopping to smell every clump of grass, every pole, every tree, and longer at his favourites – piles of sand or leaves.

I wonder along in my own trance, replaying events of the day until I realize that the sky is different. Something is happening with the moon.

I try to remember what the moon looked like yesterday. This is a full moon with a small dark crescent forming on the bottom left. I wonder if it's an eclipse, a phenomenon I have never witnessed. I haven't heard anything on the news suggesting an eclipse tonight. An old voice in my head "You never pay attention." Well I'm paying attention now.

The ocean is still, moonlight reflects across the Straight of Juan De Fuca. Although the sky is a rich black, the stars are barely visible as if they're taking a lesser role in this special play. The sounds of the neighborhood are clear and yet end their life quickly, as if giving way to a greater god.

As we walk, the shadow's progression is rapid. Within thirty minutes or so, more than three quarters of the moon has been occluded. Shortly thereafter, the eclipse is complete and the bright white light of a familiar moon, becomes a brown and orange ball standing out in the sky, as if the only one present.

With weak vision, I strain to make order out of the darker blotches on the face of the moon. This hallowed eve, I see a carved pumpkin.

> farm fields full
> of orange orbs
> children lick their lips

Fear's Thread

Walking through the forest, I duck under overhanging boughs, accidentally cut through a spider's web. The thread pulls at my face. I startle as I notice a large spider on my arm, reflexively flick it off with my finger.

As I walk on, the image replays...a beautiful creature with long legs, a tan colored body with brown spots, gracefully navigating over the pale hairs on my arm. With regret, I wish I had stifled my impulse and taken a longer look, paid more attention.

So much beauty missed because fear's reflex directed my actions.

> a silent group stands
> at graveside,
> – a robin's song

Nature Scene

A cold grey day at the tail end of the salmon run. Eagles perch in tall fir trees, swivel their heads with eyes cocked, call to let their neighbors know of their presence, and periodically swoop down to the water's edge to partake of rotting salmon carcasses.

A serious birder and I have been here for hours, shivering and reacting to any movement amongst the birds. We've each come independently to see a particular eagle that the birding community is extremely excited about – he to add the spotting to his collection, me because a friend asked me to try to get a picture of this special bird. My friend lives a thousand miles away. An avid birder himself, all he can do is follow internet conversations about the controversy – an immature and lost Asian Sea Eagle or a hybrid Bald?

Bundled into my clothing, I blow on my fingers, stomp my feet, set the camera down to clap my hands. A large eagle swoops immediately overhead – passes by to land out of sight across the bay. I scramble, grab my camera, look to the birder with a sinking feeling that I missed my chance – he purses his lips, gives a slight shake of his head. A reprieve of sorts.

Finally, I leave for home, without ever getting the desired picture, quite relieved that I didn't fail to get 'the shot'.

at the observation station
visitors point, smile, leave
– nature seen

Neighborhood Police

A plumped up Cooper exposes himself to the sun on a high branch of a tall fir. Nearby, a murder of crows raucously complains.

Intermittently, three crows rise up, circle, swoop toward the hawk. Each time, one of the three dive-bombs to within two feet of his head. Alert, the Cooper pays attention to each attack but doesn't leave his perch. On completing each assault, the crows alight with others and join in the noise.

Coopers capture small birds in flight. Their prey seldom involves crows. So why do these crows so energetically announce the threatening presence of this predator, and work so aggressively to drive him from the area? What do they have to gain?

> a visitor to our house
> steps close to me
> my dog moves between us

Summer Vacation

Seagulls float on thermals over a flat ocean. Clouds move lazily across the sky in shapes that provoke one's imagination to give them names.

At the shoreline, a great blue heron stands tall, concentrating, watching for movement below the surface. He strikes, catches a writhing eel, swings his prey in the air and in one swift motion swallows his meal. A large lump swims down the long throat. He ruffles his feathers to fling the water free, and returns to sentinel duty.

Having just started a new vacation, I compare my work-related tensions with the calm around me, take a deep breath, slow down, and wait.

> the feral cat
> back from his hunt
> a time for cleansing

A Brief Moment In Time

Inside the mouth of this long extinguished volcano, an eel slides slowly through hidden tunnels, moves from shelter to shelter. Black and white angels poke at the rocks. Green/blue parrotfish snap off pieces of corral. Pencil fish hang in suspension.

By my ear, I hear the sound of my breath in the snorkel tube, feel the chill of the water. My body rises and falls with the surge of the ocean swells.

> waves smash
> on the rough lava rock
> tiny bits of black sand

Signs of the Present

On this early winter morning, I trudge along, stressful thoughts worrying through my head. I chew the cud of things yet to be done. Then, in the forest on this well-worn path, for reasons I can't fathom, someone has dolloped white flour on the leaf-strewn ground to mark the way.

At a fork in the trail, a white arrow points to the left. Curious, I follow, head down, looking for the next sign, breathing easier now, wondering where this stranger is taking me.

At the foot of a slender tree, no different from any other tree, an X marks the spot. At first, looking up, around, down again, questioning what this is about, nothing comes but silence and my visible breath. Slowly, I realize I am alone... and that I have arrived in this particular moment.

> waning mist
> a breeze
> chills my ears

So Vivid

It's the fifth day of a seven-day fast. By intention, my daily intake has only been water with a touch of lemon. The hunger pangs mostly stopped yesterday. Today, I feel energized and alert – or at least I think I do. I avoid the group gatherings at the dinner table, and try to keep myself as quiet and relaxed as I can during normal eating times. I'm okay and the two remaining days look do-able.

However, tonight is movie night at our favourite theatre. Having paid for entry, the others dash to get their popcorn, pop, and candy. I stand off to the side, and watch. One of the patron's orders a large bag of popcorn, double butter, and a large coke. My attention is totally focused on the attendant as she collects the money, prepares the order, and places it in front of her customer.

With popcorn and pop in hand, he quickly turns to head to the theatre. As he does so, a single popped kernel, soaked in butter, lifts off the top of the pile of popcorn, floats upward for an inch or so, drifts off to the side, and slowly floats to the floor. My attention is riveted to this moment, watching every millimeter of the descent, the one bounce, and the slow roll until it comes to rest.

> spring moon
> the primrose petals
> slowly open

'Tis the Season

Arriving suddenly, their colors stand out amongst the dull brown and grey birds that hang around the feeders every day. Yellow brow patches, white stripes on black backs and wings, yellow breasts – they swarm the tree, gulping the hanging berries that have dried in the winter air.

snow flurries
festive lights
decorate the neighborhood

Evening Grosbeaks gather their dinner then depart as quickly as they came. Drunk from the fermented fruit, some bounce off our window glass, drop and rise again. Once they're gone, the usual over take the feeders.

full bellies
the turkey carcass
in the soup pot

Lingering

Stuffed head, aching muscles, fever, chills, no appetite, fatigue, draining nose – all greet me again this morning. These visitors have been with me for what seems like ten days, and show no sign of leaving.

The most that my own family can handle a visit to my home is three days. So how is it that these strangers can move in for such a long time?

eggnog
past the expiration date
work tomorrow

Noisy Anticipation

The crowd's murmur is interrupted by the first explosion of colored lights. An 'ahh' in unison welcomes the fireworks celebrating this New Year. Individual rockets sore into the night, reach their apex, then erupt as reds, whites, greens.

Exploding lights become circles, hearts, flower blossoms. Curtains of light. Separate blasts of illumination. Some lights reach higher, some drape as falling tears. Multiple explosions cascade from high, to mid to lower levels, each overlaps the others.

Each brief silence fills with applause, only to become more percussions. A longer pause. After several moments of quiet, they begin again, each series overwhelming the watchers. More 'ahhs' punctuate the explosions.

Someone says, "It's only our taxes." Talk of tight budgets didn't reach the planners who scheduled this display.

> the raucous sounds
> of the pub
> "Cheers"

A Plethora of Tulips

In deep concentration, he works in his notebook, intently drawing. His hand moves a pencil with barber pole design and a large maple leaf shaped eraser. Studying the flowers, he leans on the rock wall bordering the display, head down, face turned slightly away from me.

I'm in the feature pavilion of the Muttart Conservatory, here to shoot pictures of the wonderful array of tulips, many of which have drooping petals, petals turned inward on themselves, petals curled protectively around their stamens. I take time with each shot, capturing the lines and curves of the flowers, visually absorbing the colors, noting the perfection, and imperfections of each of my subjects.

Later when editing the images, I come across the single shot of the boy. Only now do I notice that his right ear is curled in on itself, his nose snubbed short.

> his drawing
> the curls and droops
> of his tulip

Slow Arrival

A herd of deer gathers in the field. Crows caw across the meadow. With warmer temperatures, water pools in the lower folds of land. Brown grass gives way to green. The thick surface of ice on the lake crystallizes, undulates, drifts into and away from the shore.

snow melt
the muskrat swims
his channel through the ice

Am I still young enough to feel the lust of spring.

nesting grasses
in a crow's beak
spring calls

Just Another Evening

A friend calls to tell me that a tornado warning is rolling across his TV screen, proclaiming it's imminence in my area. He urges me to take cover.

Out the window, a pleasing orange tint over the lake, scattered clouds – some white, some dark. The air is still, hot, muggy.

> mid-summer eve
> a gold finch
> at the feeder

I check the fridge for snacks.

Almost Unbearable

The weather is a noticeable visitor – hot, muggy, oppressive. The forecast calls for a string of such days, with the possibility of evening storms.

I've been suffering alone while my wife is traveling. I expect her home tonight.

hot night
the sheen of sweat
on two bodies

Lawn Slavery

blue sky, green grass
the heat
and humid air

Sweat pours off my brow, runs down the armpits of my shirt. The sun radiates heat in a blast of sunshine. The mower feels particularly heavy today. The weed beater won't kick on, despite many pulls on the starter cord. My breath is short from the exertion.

My back continues to ache. I can bend or kneel to only small degrees, for only brief moments. This should be a pleasant job, but isn't.

her job jar
still more chores
for me to do

Getting Ready

Mist rises from the large pond, creeps up the shore line and reaches the many coloured trees. Water droplets cling to the leaves – red, yellow, orange – then smack the ground as they lose their grip. Ducks paddle away from my approach, trailing vees in the water.

I'm walking alone on this rural road, wondering if I've done everything I need to do to be ready for winter. There was a forecast of possible snow last night but none fell, so there is a small reprieve.

> chest pain again
> a newly signed will
> on the table

Fall Activity

The lake is still, only minor ripples reach the shore – from the last few motorboats on their way to the ramp to be pulled from the water. Piers have been brought in, boat hoists parked on the shore. The population of our lakeside community dwindles as people return to their lives in the city.

I've done my own bit to get ready – cutting the grass for the last time, clearing the flower beds; moving the lawnmower to the back of the shed, bringing the snow blower to the front.

Leaves have changed into yellows, reds and oranges. Flocks of ducks and geese wheel off to feed in the nearby fields, seagulls congregate on the lake in noisy bunches, probably discussing when to depart for warmer weather.

> frequent visits
> to the bird feeder
> the squirrel and me

Thanksgiving

Inside, fall decorations and the glow of the fireplace warm the house. Outside, the air is moist, cool. The harvest has been gathered, combines and grain trucks parked for the year. Geese flock to the fields, find scraps of grain, build strength for their long flight south.

Beds are made, tables and chairs organized. A large turkey fills the oven. We wait for people to arrive for our family gathering.

> morning quiet
> orange light streams
> through the window

Containers of prepared food arrive with our guests, who play catch-up with each other, deal the cards, clack the backgammon tiles, go for walks, drink, argue, then finally flock to the table. Over pumpkin pie, we each share what we have to be thankful for.

> harvest moon
> a plump deer
> grazes the yard

Weekend Visit

My granddaughter arranges the pretend tea set on her little table; runs to the kitchen and fills the teapot with water; places a doll in each of the three other chairs; takes the place of honor. She carefully fills each cup, spoons in pretend sugar, pours an imagined dollop of milk.

"Drink up. This tea is yummy."

"Would you like a biscuit?"

"What are your plans for the day?"

"I miss my mommy, do you miss yours?"

"More tea? Another biscuit?"

"I feel sad. Do you?"

> mid winter
> snowed in
> an extra day

Old Man Standing

Wind rocks the evergreens, waves their branches at the passing snow. At lakeside, grey sky meets grey ice. Grey thoughts dwell on this slow end to a turbulent spring and a hesitant summer. This year feels different.

Last year, warm weather took the ice early. We got boats, piers and fishing lines into the lake with great anticipation of the coming summer.

This year, no excitement, no anticipation of warmth, no looking forward.

There's no particular reason for this melancholy – just a reaction to the drab colors, cooler than normal temperatures, living alone.

> twilight
> the coyote looks
> over his shoulder

The Small Sounds

*Silence was the small noises you heard when the larger
noises disappeared.* *

They've all left. The weekend is over. I hear creaks in the house
that weren't there during their conversations. Outside, I hear the
drip of melting snow instead of the incessant buzz of snowmobiles
racing by. The chatter of the birds is now loud enough to make me
wonder what they have to say to each other.

I'm alone with my own noises – the rumble of my guts, the beat of
my heart, the slight rasp as I breath – and my thoughts. Not much
of any significance but awareness of my being alone, wondering
what to do with my time, trolling for food.

> mmm, chocolates and sweets
> my new year pledge
> gains weight

* Robert B. Parker, The Widening Gyre, 1983, Dell Publishing,
New York.

Red Sand

red sand
footsteps at the water supply
of an ancient people

Hiking a cottonwood wash in Arches National Park within the red rock country of Utah, we approach a wet area that surrounds a deep stagnant pool. In the wet soil, a lens cap catches my eye, I stoop to pick it up, notice it's a Nikon and think my friend has passed by this spot. She has a history of dropping her lens caps. To the left, I see a clear sloping path through the bush and step onto the rich, wet red soil.

red sand
this dry dessert
drinks from the pool

I slip, my left foot flies in the air, my right hand reaches to grab a non-existent support, my head falls back. I land on my right hip, slide down the short slope and gasp for the breath that was knocked out of me as my back followed my hip. A moment, a hand down in the wet sand, a knee pressed into the red mud, and I slowly stand. I collect myself, check out my gear.

red sand
the mud between my fingers
thousands of years old

Red on my hand, pants, shirt back, camera and face. My own lens cover was in my pocket so now my lens is mostly occluded by rich, red Utah mud. The back of my camera is coated in thick red goo. My backpack, which absorbed the heavy blow of much of my weight, is smeared. Slowly, I move on, follow my comrade.

red sand
many untaken photos,
now only mental images

30 cm in the Forecast

empty winter boots
a raven at the feeder
quorks his 'thank you'

Magpies and Blue Jays compete for nuts and seeds in the bird feeder. Chickadees wait for the big boys to leave. Snow falls steadily. The shed, fence, car, the walk and lawn catch and hold the white flakes. The snow inches higher. The temperature slowly drops.

snow drifts
my lottery numbers
match so far – three to go

The shed door is open. A new snow blower sits at the entrance, ready for its first use. Too big for what has fallen but prepared for what is coming, it sits idle as I continue to gauge the depth.

melting snow
drips from my parka
coffee and a warm fire

Red Sand Revisited

I sit to attempt a cleaning of my lens and camera body, still coated in a dried crust of red Utah mud – now a tough, almost ceramic coating. I use a pick and brushes to dislodge the bulk of the crusted sand, but carefully on the lens so as not to scratch the glass surface. Glass cleaner and a rag finally remove the evidence that I wiped out, collapsed on my prat, and messed up my clothing and gear.

Tonight, I share my photos from that trip.

in front of an audience
showing photos
of Utah rock formations
a befuddled speech
about red sand

Night Drive

Stars shinning in a black sky, lights in my windshield and rear view mirror, my only companions are the truckers hauling their loads across the country on Highway 84 – an economic lifeline as goods move south east or north west.

I play my CD's, eat my sunflower seeds to stay awake, and feel the vibration of the tires. I enjoy the solitude, the ease with which the miles pass, and the feeling of being part of a living organism moving steadily forward.

> truck stop coffee
> and conversation
> Oregon wagon train

What is He Thinking?

The pond is a quiet place, seldom disturbed by human interlopers. I've come here on a windless summer day to clear my mind. I sit quietly, focus on my breathing. Suddenly, the whoosh of large wings as a heron swoops into the clearing, settles into the shallows.

For long minutes, he simply stands tall, immovable, focused. Periodically, he takes a slow, prolonged step; stirs the muddy bottom as he shifts; alertly watches for any signs of movement.

I envy this quiet state; compare my active mind with his stillness. But perhaps I give him too much credit. Is this heron as busy thinking as I am? Does he worry that this pond has been completely fished out? Does he fret about how the leeches don't taste as good as the frogs? Maybe he worries he'll only catch a small leech, if he catches anything at all? Perhaps, he thinks to himself "Was that a movement? It was, wasn't it? I know it was a movement. I missed it. Damn!"

> lucky bird
> whatever happens
> just happens

Note: This piece emerged after reading Time With the Heron by Jeffrey Woodward, which he included in his collection of haibun and haiku titled Evening in the Plaza: Haibun and Haiku.

Reflections

Some momentary observations induced me to reflect on some aspect of myself – my past and how it affected me, how I choose to live my life, how current moments affect me and trigger other thoughts, what is to become of me. These haibun typically use present tense language to describe a moment and then relate to something in my basic nature. I use the observation to reflect on self then share that with you.

Morning Voices

Malaise greets me in the morning as I shift out of bed. The old, early morning voice, 'Get up and greet the world' is missing from my head. I no longer wake with a sense of hope, a readiness to make the world – my world – a better place.

> a banana slug
> inches along
> distant footsteps

Age is a factor but no real excuse – many people age, still enthuse about their adventure. An older friend lives in the moment, monks about, writes poetry, seduces the ladies. A second chases birds of another feather around the countryside. A third prunes plants, listens to the nearby trickle of water and buzzing insects. A fourth speaks to the spirits of ancient ancestors, feels her inner peace.

Me, I feel alone, empty, no longer of use to myself, to others. My inner child gone, sleeping, hiding, dead?

> as the axe cuts,
> chips fly
> a missing companion

Cowardice is more likely the culprit. Indecision, an unwillingness to act, eats up energy like a sun-dried sponge sucks up pooled water. This knowing what needs to be done and not doing it melts my spirit.

> fading light
> wax dribbles
> down the candle stem

Ah, but look at me. Heavy words on paper that don't seem real.

> a child's voice
> threads through the noise
> "I'm still here!"

The Turn

Yesterday

A visit to the Dean's new office. Desk piled high, books scattered about the room, un-hung pictures rest on the floor. In casual clothes, he invites me to sit while he sorts through his documents. I note that my chair is lower than his so I have to look up to make eye contact.

He hesitantly broaches the subject of our meeting. We're here to discuss student evaluations for my last course. I expect the worst. It was my first time back in front of an academic class in twenty years, and I know it did not go well.

The scores are low, the comments harsh and judgmental, descriptions of my behaviour both accurate and unflattering. The severity of the comments surprises me but their concerns do not. I share their disappointment.

> a corn maze twists,
> turns, dead ends
> the crunch of brittle leaves

I slink to my car, head for the safety of home.

Today

I wake fresh with ideas and a burning desire to get to my computer to put a new course plan into words. My fingers hunt, peck, bang the percussive beat that accompanies the flow of thoughts. I spread ideas out on the page, cut, sort, slash away thoughts that don't keep up. Student complaints morph into permissions to abandon old ways, to innovate, to feel excitement about new activities.

> sunshine through the trees
> a chickadee lands
> even as the feeder fills

I send the new design to the Dean by e-mail, wait for him to share my excitement.

64

Neglected Duties

Three nights in a row, sleep came very late. I've been in the 9th century amongst warriors, clergy and kings.

This damn book series has captured my attention and just won't let go. Time passes without my awareness. I flip page after page, eagerly searching for what happens to these characters that have become my friends and enemies. I wake in the morning, tired, too compelled to get back to the words on the page.

And what is this escape into another reality all about? The many deaths in the book provoke my own grief. The heroic feats touch my own fantasies of the superhero I wanted to be. The crowd of characters reduces my loneliness. The doggedness of the common people strikes a chord with the survivor in me.

> newspaper on the doorstep
> the empty dog bowl
> skitters across the floor

To Worry Or Not To Worry

Despite the trappings of an elder, I'm still a scared little boy living in a man's body, generally constraining my life to safe, warm places. Self-doubt scares me away from adventure. I consistently anticipate what can go wrong, justify this state of mind as being prepared for disaster.

I visit Mexico on a rare vacation. Barely dressed children roam the streets, yet have smiles on their faces as they play with whatever junk they find. They walk barefoot on cobble stone streets, carry their chickens as playmates, dash around parked cars, wade in shallow pools of stagnant water.

I wonder, "Would I have been better off having such a childhood?" They seem fearless.

old house
a sleepless child
counting monsters

Where are the Birds?

silence today
hoarfrost outside
and a warm fire inside

My cupboards and refrigerator have all the food I need. My car has sufficient gasoline. My roof is waterproof. Insulated walls keep me warm even in the coldest of weather. The plumbing works. Cable delivers hundreds of TV channels to satisfy any taste. The library lets me borrow as much as I can read. I regularly visit with those who are important to me.

However, I've isolated myself from the horrors of the world and live quietly in my middle class. I stay away from daily news where people do each other harm.

As a recluse, I feel too small to even attempt to make a difference. I leave the world to it's own problems and take care of my own.

30^0 below
no seeds
in the bird feeder

The Flight Of A Promise

Sitting upright in an airplane seat that won't recline, I drift into brief sleep, wake to the sudden sense of falling. Fear takes my breath. Instantly, I replay the opening of a recent movie, which showed the last moments of an airplane flight that ended in tragedy.

> air pockets
> the movie
> stops in mid scene

I've made a commitment to my daughter and her daughter, taking on an important role in their lives, and feel the need to live as long as I can. That promise rises in my throat as the plane suddenly jars, bounces about.

> above the clouds
> the calm voice of the pilot
> offers assurances

The plane levels out into smooth flight. Breathing easier, I remind myself there is more risk driving my car or walking the streets than there is flying on a commercial airline.

> smooth touch down –
> the drive home
> uneventful

Paradise Lost — or Found?

I've just moved back to the prairies.

On the island paradise that I just left, life was easy. We lived a quiet life of retirement in a climate that caressed mind, soul and body – moist cool air in the winter, body temperature drought in the summer. Our days were green, slow paced affairs. To folks that didn't make the move, we bragged about the wonder of living in this place, a home in which we would live out the rest of our lives.

Now, that paradise is the place of a grave to tend. My partner of 43 years lies in the ground of her choosing.

Me – I'm a long way away. I'm here now in the city of my youth, come to be with family. I'm to be a nanny for my new granddaughter – to watch the cycle of life from another point of view, to draw warmth through loving a child.

> ducks and geese
> gather on the lake
> an early autumn

I'm Home.

I've just returned to live in the Alberta city of my youth. It's summer now. The sunlight, the temperature of the air, the open terrain of prairie fields mostly feel right – feel as they should, feel as I've known them for most of my life. The smell of the countryside comes to me as an old friend, especially around the wide-open sloughs with waterfowl splitting the waters, shorebirds beaking the muck, blackbirds screaming about their territory.

I visit old, easy-to-be-with friends – easy because the angst of bonding has taken its leave, making room for our comfortable openness. The familiar says I'm home.

I know that harsh winter will come – deep freeze weather, square wheels on cars, hoarfrost on windows, parkas so large they don't fit in our coat closets, double time to get anywhere. But that anticipation feels familiar as well.

> early freeze-up
> geese circle south
> while squirrels gather food

The Prohibition

> coming night
> nervous men in line
> at the red-light door

In the photo taken in 1930, five are seated in a parlor with a large mirror, a naked statue draped with flowing cloth, a snake on the arm of the lamp with a large white shade. Four in white, one in black, their best dresses flow onto the floor, bosoms emphasized, plump or otherwise. Hair done up in the style of the early nineteen hundreds, cosmetics shade their cheeks, necklaces highlight their bare necks.

Posing but not smiling, ready for work, this is a full-service brothel. Men of a particular persuasion would ask for the "lady" in black, a smorgasbord of white for the other good citizens. The Madam, pariah of the town, donates the most to charity.

I'm reminded that as a virginal young man, I contemplated sneaking in to learn what I could about sex; but shame, embarrassment, fear, critical judgment kept me away. If I had visited, would I have chosen the lady second from the left?

> a monk writes
> about a geisha's beauty
> "magnolia in bloom"

* This haiku relates to a haiku attributed to Basho at Bashorcvisitcd.blogspot.ca

> Ah! such a beauty
> the white face of a geisha
> magnolia in bloom

Two Paces Forward, One Back

After a stormy spell, this early summer weather has just taken a turn for the better. Things are drying up; the wind has declined to a breeze, just ruffling the leaves; whitecaps have become ripples on the lake surface. The first long weekend is over, leaving quiet and solitude. With a contented sigh, I turn to my e-mail.

A friend writes about his disquiet over the meaning of his life – lacking a clear sense of purpose in his 70s. I identify with his words.

I'm now a consumer of life, no longer producing anything of value to others. I eat, exercise, take pleasure in recreational activity, read, watch too much TV, spend hours in my car getting from one place to the other, sleep.

> still morning
> the buzz of my thoughts
> won't stop

Deepest Potential?

Recently and coincidentally, some of my reading, television viewing, and movie watching have touched on the history of the Second World War, and particularly the actions of the Nazis, and the suffering of those they placed in concentration camps, or abused in public life.

Never having been tested by any form of serious hardship, or any surrounding threat to life, I'm amazed at how people adjusted to the everyday horrors of the period. I'm equally shocked by the dastardly acts that human beings could perpetrate on others, and the apparent ease with which such heinous behavior could be rationalized and justified.

I wonder about my own capacity for survival in such trying times. Could I have survived the holocaust? Would I have had what it takes to tolerate such pain?

In turn, I also wonder what atrocities I might have committed if living in the same circumstances. I like to think I have the strength and conviction to hold to humane values, but never having been tested, don't really know.

> quiet day
> a jackfish fights
> the treble hook

Not An Every Day Hero

Why is it that I'm so into reading novels with heroes like Jack Reacher, Eric Cole, Joe Pike, Walt Longmire* – strong silent types afraid of nothing, willing to risk their lives for the sake of justice, protectors of the vulnerable. Stronger, faster, more agile than their opponents – they walk into danger without anxiety or trepidation. They stand tall, face death, and win.

I guess its because they're everything I'm not, but wish I could be. I'm old, overweight, stiff and sore, slow when I move, and prone to worry. I feel for the underdog, abhor injustice, but don't have the skill set to do much good.

> a crow on the edge
> of a robin's nest
> a parent's squawk

* Characters in novels by Lee Child, Robert Crais, and Craig Johnson.

Lost Innocence

Today, I pick my granddaughter up at daycare. She sees me, yells "Grumps", drops what she's holding, and runs toward me. I get down on one knee, eye level. She rushes up, holds nothing back and gives me a full body hug. Several other children rush in to join in one great big group hug. My granddaughter whispers – "We call this a sandwich hug".

Also today, I meet some long time male friends for dinner. We greet each other with hugs – sort of. For one, a handshake becomes a lean forward and a shoulder bump; with another, single arms reach over each other's shoulder. With the third, I exchange a timid chest bump; and with the fourth, we each extend a single arm around the other's back and give a gentle pat.

I'm struck by the difference – when did I get so uptight about showing my joy when greeting my friends?

finger painting
a teacher says
"that's not how to do it."

outdoor hockey rink
gay slurs and jokes
in the locker room

the command from
HIS easy chair
"Come here, give me a hug!"

once best friends
only hesitant eye contact
after many years

Relationships

In some cases, my haibun refer to how I'm dealing with a relationship with another person in my life. These relationships include family members, friends, or colleagues from some venture I've been on.

Her Birthday

The University student lounge, noisy… crowded. I sport a large goose egg and stitches over my brow, a football injury from the night before. I feel dour, look miserable.

As I search for a place within this chaos to place my food and eat my lunch, a friend calls me over. He occupies a booth with four strangers. I squeeze in, exchange hellos, and receive a chorus of "What the hell did you do to yourself?".

Today is the birthday of one of the women, and they want to celebrate. I look at her for the first time. I'm struck by her excitement, by her 'take charge' approach as she organizes their party.

She laughs at someone's tease about sharing a birth date with Winston Churchill. I notice her smile.

How can I explain? Her smile holds me just as captive today, as if it was Winston's birthday forty years ago – and I have the scars to prove it.

> photos in my box
> her face
> still radiant

Her Fight

Early morning: the hum of the fridge, the purr of the furnace, the slight tick of plant leaves brushing each other as air rises from the floor vents. This crowded home has yet to rise for the day. I sit on the steps that rise up into a raised living room. Thoughts drift.

In the kitchen, cupboard doors open and close. With heavy footfalls, one of the other adults enters the kitchen. In a gruff voice, he shouts, "Get off the countertops! You know you're not supposed to be up there!" Without hesitation, a little girl's voice replies, "You're not the boss of me! I have a right to get my stuff too."

She storms to the living room, plunks herself down on one of the steps, her elbows on her knees, drops her chin into her hands, and frowns. I feel her steaming energy as she broods.

I ask, "Having a real fight eh?".

Curtly, "Yeah – he won't let me get my stuff."

"Want my help?"

"No! … It's my fight!"… and my four year old marches sternly back into the kitchen – and into the rest of her life.

> flower blossom
> the deer stares down
> a barking dog

Old Couple

Following an argument with my wife, I walk over to the park, sit on a picnic table to think.

The dense bushes form a wall at the far end of the field. An old couple works together, as each reaches into the green and picks lush blackberries. Silent, busy at their work, they toil beside each other, filling their buckets.

I wonder what their relationship has been – peaceful, strained, open and intimate, or strangers in the same bed. Has theirs been like mine – an unfinished movie with good scenes and bad, high points and moments of boredom, growing together and growing apart.

> a long journey
> on old tires,
> full buckets of berries

Movies Not Seen

I've been gone only two weeks and she was nine months old when I left.

Since – she has had her first bout of illness; learned to actually crawl on all fours, not just commando crawl; and, she developed the ability to pull herself up into a full, self-maintained sitting position.

Momentous experiences and I missed them.

> old man
> the photo album
> only half full

Our Walk

I click on 'Save', send the first draft to my hard drive. I've been working for much of the morning. I turn and ask if he'd like to go for our usual walk through the forest. As I expect, he leaps up, looks at me with an intense stare. Reading his gestures, I know his thoughts – "Of course, you fool, let's go."

"Whoops" I say as a new idea comes to me. I turn to my keyboard, add the thought to my document, edit a sentence that comes before. To me, it's only seconds. In reality, five minutes become ten, and more. Out of the corner of my eye, I see and hear him grumble to himself, plunk back down, hang his head. It's a safe bet he's upset, thinking negative thoughts, "Sucked in again."

Feeling guilty, I save the document, say "Sorry about that. Let's go." In anger, he replies with a "Yup!", quickly heads for the door. I figure he doesn't want to give me a chance to change my mind.

As I put on my boots, he paces back and forth, looks out the window, then looks at me as if to say, "What the hell is taking so long?"

Once out the door, I have to walk quickly to keep up. I know this is his favourite walk, but I can only guess why. I'm thinking this is something ancestral for him.

He runs ahead, barks out, "Let's go, Let's go!", charges into the forest, leaving me well behind.

> scent ahead
> checking out rotting logs,
> damp earth, scuttling animals

Through the Mist

A camera club excursion. Heavy fog surrounds the pier, moored boats, and the city of houseboats at Fisherman's wharf. Rust, peeled paint, disorganized rope lines dumped on boat decks tell the tale of a closed fishery. The salmon didn't come this year.

Each of us works alone, searches for winning images, keeps our secrets. In shame, I keep to myself for another reason. I behaved badly in an argument with one of our club members.

He approaches nonchalantly, tripod slung over his shoulder, camera and long lens suspended in his large hand. "Hello" he says as if nothing had happened between us to make it strange to speak to each other. His eyes seek my answer.

I "hi" back, comment on the great turnout. He chats on about how great it is to have thick fog this morning, says this is one of his favourite places to visit with his camera.

> fishermen, once competitors,
> sit, talk away the time –
> coffee warms cold hands

Just Grazing

Late at night, few on the road, I work to keep from nodding off. An empty tank and a full bladder drive me into the gas station. I fill up, rush inside for relief. On the way out, I grab a giant chocolate bar to spike my energy for the long drive.

"That'll be $3.35." she says. I hand her a five. "$1.65" as she places the change in my palm and our hands lightly touch. Eye contact ... a nod .... and ...... I head for the truck.

> Ooh…high beams
> two deer nuzzle
> on the edge of the road

Littered Path

The whistle of the wind. The thrum of a gust that bends tall trees. The knock of an Arbutus trunk against a fir. The sharp snap deep in the forest that may be a tree breaking. Broken branches scatter about the forest floor.

Disturbed from his perch in a smaller tree, a humming bird ascends, hovers, dives into the safety of a sturdy old Douglas.

On my walk home from work, I lean into the wind, think about our fight last night.

> note on the table
> "I'm leaving for good…
> this time"

Gathering Of The Guys

At least three months since we last got together, the four of us trickle in to the house of our host, share awkward hugs, say "how're you doing", ask one how his trip to Maui was, another about his work in Pincher Creek, tell a third about a currently running movie that he should see. Steaks are thrown into pans on the stove top, sizzling as they strike hot iron. International beers are talked about and shared as we slowly settle into eating.

Jim, who had a tough year with the passing of three of his family members, says "I think about death every day. I wake up, notice that I'm still here, and then I think about what I'll do with my remaining time."

Bob, as he often does, quotes one of his mentor's in the men's movement, "At the moment of death, you'll be thinking 'Did I love well enough?'"

Sid quickly replies: "I don't think that's what I'll be thinking. Maybe 'Did I live well enough?'"

Fred says, "I don't think that's what would be going through my head either. I don't know what I'd be thinking about."

And I sit there quietly, pondering that thought. Will my last thoughts be in turmoil, fighting against the dark? I don't have a religious framework that props me up, no vision of a hereafter. I can't imagine myself wondering if I loved or lived well enough. I just lived.

But in this sober moment, I aspire to more hopeful thoughts – to be in the moment, to have an open mind to the experience, and if I slip out of that moment, perhaps I'll wonder, "What's next?"

> a deep sigh
> interrupts the silence
> then a burp

Parenting Stories

The phone call, words coming between sobs and choked breathing – my daughter, mother of my seven-month-old granddaughter Quynn, admits to a terrible mistake.

She paints the picture with her words – Quynn, in a Bumbo seat on the kitchen countertop, having her breakfast, squirming about, reaching over the sides of the seat trying to pick things up. Mom, turning back from putting food in the fridge, sees Quynn launch herself, falling face first, heading toward the floor. My daughter leaps, catches her, just as she goes over the edge of the counter top.

Upon hearing how upset my daughter is, I flash on one of my own parental mistakes – one that involved her. Close to Quynn's age, she lies on the top bunk bed as I change her. Dirty diaper in hand, I bend over to the diaper pail. She rolls herself to the edge of the bunk bed, falls to a heavy thud on the floor. I grab her up, both of us in shock, tears and cries of anguish. Fortunately, nothing damaged but our feelings.

In reply to my daughter's anguish on the phone, I remind her about our own incident, relate how I felt the air sucked out of me when she fell, felt a terrible fear about what could have happened, experienced incredible quilt and self-criticism over letting this happen, and then, when we both settled down, realized anxious relief that she was okay.

I ask if she felt the same way after her daughter's fall. She says, "It was more horrible than that!"

I remind her that at least she didn't let her daughter hit the floor.

> bankruptcy
> jokes about being okay
> after the collapse

An Awkward Hug

After a year's separation and a couple thousand miles of driving from two sides of the continent, two buddies greet each other. One reaches out his hand, the other opens his arms. Tentative, awkward, each trying to figure out whose head and arms go where, the handshake becomes a hug, stirs memories.

> a dandelion ball
> shudders in the wind
> a few seeds stir

"Come on, give your dad a kiss goodnight." he says. With trepidation, the boy steps forward, embraces his father's neck, kisses a stubbled cheek. Memories of unexpected wrath, punishments that hurt, moil amongst a young boy's wishes to please, to earn his father's love.

> old memories
> when he approaches,
> the dog cringes

Dedication of a Champion

Like the postman, neither wind, snow, sleet nor rain keeps him from his work. Many years, all four seasons kayaking on white water, training for the next major race. Run the course, work to shave hundredths of seconds, pull the kayak from the river and walk back to start again. Under the watchful eye of his coach, he paddles toward criticism and correction. Forget what is comfortable, push into behavior that feels strange. Learn a new skill to replace the old.

> golden dreams
> this river flows
> faster and faster

> bleak news
> a parent worries
> about a son's choices
> to take
> a certain path

Failure first, success later. He has to learn to lose like a champion to be able to win like one. Words of encouragement from the world's current champion become a mantra for winning.

> a dream
> only a dream
> until you make it happen

> realities
> the old man
> talks about the future
> and the need to
> earn a living

Slowly, his turn comes. A third place finish in a world cup race becomes ta gift to a father who is proud whether he wins or loses.

He frames the medal with a photograph of him in his kayak crossing the finish line and presents it to a man he thanks as an inspiration for effort and dedication. He has it wrong – he has become the model to be emulated.

More medals follow, bronze, silver, then gold.

> changing dreams
> the nuances of moving water
> now more important

> lumpy couch
> an old man sits,
> watches a race on TV,
> worries
> about his son

His work intensifies as he chases the prize he covets – the trophy of a world champion. Travel to countries where the guards in airports have machine guns, where the temperatures average above 40 degrees centigrade, where the audiences exceed any for a race at home, he races in the European countries where world champions typically come from.

Then one day, a parental call to ask how he's doing.

> a brilliant day
> an interloper
> succeeds
> and a new champion
> is crowned

> quiet night
> an old man
> has proud dreams

Unexplainable Connections

Late in life, we've become friends – open and generous with each other, sharing the aftermath of our new widowhood after many years of marriage. We grieve together, moan about the financial predicament of having our bank accounts frozen on the death of a spouse, discuss our loneliness, and over time apprehensively joke about what it would be like to get back into the dating game.

And then…. we each find a new mate. He turned to a friend from childhood. I turned to a friendship shared with my wife over the past thirty years. We surprise ourselves by our similarities… given our differences.

It amazes me that I, a relative recluse, found this friend at this ripe old age, and yet he feels as familiar as a brother.

> parallel lines
> center the road
> two travelers

Minor Calamity

"Hey, Grumps – it's wet." says my granddaughter.

I pull the washing machine out to find a large puddle of water, and spit a curse … she looks at me, dashes to the couch to watch some TV.

A mop, towels – the wringing fills a bucket with water. I search for the source but don't find an obvious leak. The other day, they'd hooked up a new well, with a new pressure system. Thinking that the pressure might be set too high, I push the button to bring it down.

I run the washing machine while it is pulled forward from the wall, hoping that a gush of water will reveal the problem.

> oh oh – is that a skunk
> slinking into the bush –
> no, just fluttering leaves

Relieved that no new flooding occurs, I put everything back in its place, prepare our dinner, and settle my feelings.

> sink full of dishes
> she sneaks up
> and gives me a hug

Coming Together

I'm sixty-six, a widower from a 43 year marriage. After her departure and my grieving, I looked forward with loathing to the dating process. I had failed at that game as a kid, and hadn't really played in many years. A history of a few clumsy affairs before and during the marriage left me shy and unsure – socially and sexually.

I know I can live comfortably on my own, but I don't want to.

> morning
> the snail crosses
> the walkway

She's a fifty-eight year old divorcé from an adulterous marriage. Thrust into independent living with damaged self-esteem, she worked hard to re-build confidence and comfort as a single adult. She too feels awkward and less than confident in the dating game.

She knows she can live comfortably on her own, but she doesn't want to.

> solitary tree
> billboards on the roadside
> promote a new lifestyle

We know we can live comfortably, each on our own, but we don't want to.

> afternoon heat
> ice cream on sale
> in the nearby grocery store

The Season For Giving

The letter from a long time friend is a request for a donation to support her coming political campaign. Her hand written note tells me that she still believes passionately in her party's goals, believes she and her party can make the world a better place. She's gotten bolder with her ask, suggesting larger amounts. She wants to win.

I'm disheartened, no longer convinced I can make a difference, realize the heavy consequence of retirement – going from an income to only 'outgo'.

> crumpled bank statement
> my Christmas gift list
> just got longer

No Thank You

On the morning that we leave on our five-week RV trip, for the first time I hand her the keys to what has been 'my' motorhome. Giving her the keys feels like a big act on my part, another step in our new partnership. I have never let someone else drive. She has expressed a desire to take the wheel, but I've been afraid of how she would do in heavy traffic.

Thinking that we are departing on a quiet lakeside roadway, I figure she will have a bit of time to get comfortable driving this big rig before she reaches the highway. We're leaving early in the day. I've foolishly picked a morning that is still dark, and we're starting out on what I have to admit is a narrow road closed in by overhanging trees, with snow on the road edges.

> misty morning
> a deer noses
> into the meadow

Worried about how close she comes to the passenger side ditches, I urge her to drive more to her left. I know she is nervous about the size of this vehicle, but tell her it is like driving her van. Within a few miles, she pulls to the side of the road, stops the engine, silently hands me the keys, and gives me a hard stare.

> today's long drive
> a pillow and blanket
> on the couch

Our Place No Longer

For many years, in June and September, the four of us visited this rustic cabin on the shores of Lake Edith in Jasper National Park. Last fall, the owners placed it on the market.

> winter wind
> the 'for sale' sign
> tattered and bleached

The front windows face over the lake with snow covered Mount Edith Cavell in the distance. Reflections of clouds dance on the water, riffles from the wind gently move the canoe tied at the end of the pier.

Still cool this June, the old fireplace burns and crackles. Each of us reads, or processes the photographs taken on one of our many hikes. Music from our large collection plays in the background. Conversations break out when some image or song stirs a thought, a memory, a feeling. One of us says "I hope the cabin will still be available in the fall."

> barren trees
> cabin doors locked
> and "SOLD"

Spring Thaw

The thick cover of snow on the old fir slowly melts. A crocus pokes from dark soil in the cone of the tree. Low flying geese swoop over the lake and break the silence.

> morning after
> her cold shoulder
> warming to the touch

He's Late.

His pattern has always been to arrive on time, or more typically, be the first to arrive. The four of us sit at the table with food on our plates, nibbling but not really eating, assuming he will walk in the door any minute. After ten minutes, we wonder if he's had a mishap and worry about his wellbeing. I call.

After three rings, he answers "Hello Gary", having seen caller ID before answering. I ask where he is and if he's all right. He says, "I'm not coming. I sent an e-mail but I guess you haven't had a chance to read it yet. I don't feel safe in the group. I don't feel connected. I'm dropping out." I ask if I can put him on speakerphone so the others can hear and he says I should just tell them, says goodbye and hangs up.

The four of us sit silently. He has just dropped out of a group in which he's been a member for about eight years. We each speak of our reaction – surprise, sadness, disappointment, some anger that he didn't come to tell us of his feelings in a face-to-face gathering, some wondering about what he meant about not feeling safe in our discussions.

The group proceeds without him. We each check-in, share information about our own wellbeing and emotional states, talk about the questions and issues that we struggle with on a day-to-day basis.

> his absence
> deep, personal
> sharing

One Sick Kid

A temperature of 103°, a flaming red throat, and deep dark sacks under her eyes, she can't go to school and needs minding.

I get the call, rush into the city to look after my granddaughter. This has happened before, and I welcome the chance to be there.

On arrival, I'm advised the fever is under control for now. She took some Tylenol just after I was called but it's obvious she's very sick. She barely looks up to acknowledge my presence, takes no note of her mother's leaving for a weeklong conference in another city.

I sit close beside her. She cuddles up against me, dozes. I feel the fever slowly returning.

> stormy night
> disturbed dreams
> of sick and dying children

Later, after she has recovered, she asks, "How come my mom always goes away when I'm sick?"

Spontaneous Teamwork

As I drive the boat across the lake, the pontoons crash through the four-foot swells and the boat is pushed off course by wind and wave action.

On arrival at the boat launch, I see that my partner has backed the trailer down the boat ramp, close to a floating pier, hoping that it will provide a breakwater. Unused to backing up the trailer, she has placed it at a diagonal into the water. I now have a narrow channel within which to accomplish my approach, and the need to somehow use boat, wind, and wave power together to hit the narrow runnels on the trailer where the keels of each pontoon have to ride.

The front end lines up fine and rises onto the trailer as it should, but the boat is large and clumsy and the wave action swings the back end off the trailer – half on, half off, and no likelihood that we will fix the problem. I back off and try again. Once…. twice.

Bystanders, both amused and growing impatient by our predicament, give directions and urge us on. Finally, a stranger volunteers, pulls the truck forward, backs the trailer down the ramp, tailing directly out into the lake.

I nose up to the trailer. Along with my partner, this stranger leaps into chest deep water, grabs a rope, muscles the boat against the current and lines up the front. I scramble overboard; push the back end so it tracks properly onto the runnels. Once in position, our good Samaritan grabs the winch line, hooks it to the boat and cranks, the ratchet clicking away as the boat inches forward.

> sighs and laughter
> already thinking of next year,
> and a calmer day

A Touch Of Loneliness

an albatross in flight
thousands of miles
over deep dark sea

Trees wave in the breeze, sway, touch each other. Geese herd their
fresh goslings by brushing against them. Three fox kits emerge
from a nearby culvert, cuddle together, watch as I walk by.
Millions of Mayflies brush my face and hum in ecstasy as they rise
and fly against each other.

a warm blanket
this batch of puppies
scrambles over each other

An old AT&T advertisement said, "Reach out and touch
someone." That never quite worked for me. Calling someone on a
phone wasn't quite touching the person I was speaking with. I
couldn't see, smell, or taste them either, but most noticeably, I
couldn't reach out and feel them, or experience their touch on me.
Hearing them, and being able to share something of myself was
better than total loneliness but it wasn't intimacy either.

abandoned outhouse
no warm butts
on cold seats

I now live in a rural setting, a lakeside house, where there are few
people still around. Today, I'm feeling the loneliness. So who do I
reach out for now? Phone or e-mail?

an old friend
stories remembered,
shared with laughter

Okay, all whining aside, it will do.

Seven Pillows!

She just acquired a new-to-her RV, a converted Chevy Van she has named Strider. I'm her Bilbo, and with my wife's permission, along to provide moral support and relevant skills. She needs to learn how to use her unit, how the electrical and propane systems work, how to camp in both serviced parks and boondocking situations, how to cook in tight spaces, and how to drive a unit much larger than her small car. It will be my job to show her how to do this.

> many firsts
> new places to visit
> marked on the map

I have my own, much larger motorhome in which we travelled together several times, each with our own sleeping quarters and with lots of room to move about. However, on this adventure, it is parked at home. We journey forth, heading for places we haven't yet visited, facing the quandary, how will we share the tight space of her van.

> wheels on the road
> sardines packed tighter
> than when they swam free

Good and close friends for over thirty years, our relationship is about to be put to a test. The first night is a chilly one. She brought along plenty of bedding so we shouldn't be cold but the sleeping arrangement works against warmth.

For propriety's sake, sleeping head to foot on an almost queen size bed, she keeps pulling covers away from my side and exposes my feet to the cold night air. I curl up to keep warm, a sleeping posture I don't like very much, while trying to minimize the amount of bed space I occupy. Being ultra careful, we avoid touching each other. She is surrounded by seven full size pillows and cocooned in two comforters. I have a sheet.

> this old man tosses,
> turns through the night
> an early sunrise

We discuss the situation the next morning. I slept poorly. She's quite pleased with her first night in her new van. We agree we can work out a more comfortable arrangement for both of us, have a cold breakfast, and move on down the road. We arrive at an old abandoned mining town where we will boondock for the night.

> town jailhouse
> vigilantes hung 102 men
> in three months

We spend the evening taking pictures of the town buildings and, finally as darkness settles in, arrange the bed so we are sleeping head to head. Her mountain of pillows and the overly large and thick comforters protect her and I sleep as tightly packed along the wall of the van as I can, occupying less than 20 inches of the width of the bed. For most of the night, I have no awareness that she is sleeping next to me.

> temperatures drop
> inside the van
> more disturbed sleep

In the early hours of a below freezing morning, I hear, "I'm cold." I shift over, move bedding aside, lay back-to-back, share body heat. My inner voices prevent further sleep.

"Hmm. This feels good."

"I'm married,. What am I thinking?"

"We've been platonic friends for years, travelled together, have never been intimate, we're not going to start now."

"Damn. She's a woman, I'm a man.... Oh, just be cool."

"Good, we're getting warmer. This will be okay. We're just keeping each other warm."

"I'm not really being naughty, am I? What will happen when I tell my wife?"

After a couple of hours, she wakes, gets up, acts as if nothing significant has happened. It would seem that she had none of the inner tension that kept me awake, and that she got what she wanted – a good sleep on a cold night. Once again, we hit the road on our journey to meet friends and take more pictures.

an uneventful journey
new places visited
with old friends

Afterwards

At six this morning, the gunshot of thunder immediately followed a bright lightning strike. Rain broke from the skies. The pellets of rain percussed the roof of our motorhome for a solid hour, then became the steady rasp of a light drizzle. Slowly, silence grows as the rain turns to large flakes of snow settling on the surrounding tents, trailers, motorhomes, tables and trees. Flakes in communion now fall in wet clumps.

> the furnace kicks on
> and warm air fills the space
> no sign of our squirrel

We, the people in the campground, cloister in our tents, trailers and motorhomes waiting for summer to return. After an hour of snow, there's a knock on the door. "We need help. The heavy snow is dragging down the tarps and awnings."

I rush out to other campsites to find ropes stretched, sagging tarps full of snow, ghost like shapes as they lean on the lawn chairs beneath them. We pitch in to get the snow removed, and the tarps untied so they can fall to the ground and drop the snow. We move through the campground dropping awnings to half-mast, sweeping off the heavy wet snow, careful to not tear the cloth.

> a constant stream of snow
> hot chocolate and s'mores
> around the evening fire

Commentary

In some cases, when reading or hearing stories and information from others, I'm stimulated to write about my reaction to what I've learned. This is not typically done in the haibun genre but I have sometimes used this writing style to express myself. In sharing such haibun, I suppose I reveal something of my prejudices, opinions, and outlook on the world.

Remembrance Day

Today's paper has two very interesting stories.

The first is a profile of a wartime veteran who received the Victoria Cross for valor on the battle field in World War II. For heroic acts risking his own life multiple times, he received the highest award given to soldiers of the British Commonwealth. However, today's story was about how surviving members of his family, sixty years later and now destitute, had to sell that medal to gain money to live on.

The second story covers the strike in the National Hockey League. A recent meeting of the striking players concluded with a reaffirmation of the solidarity of their union. It seems that they universally agree to continue to hold out against the owners of the teams. The average player receives $1.8 million dollars in salary per year. They strike to preserve those earnings in the face of the owners saying that the league will fail financially unless controls on player's salaries are put in place. Ticket prices are at such a level that most people can't afford to attend the games.

I wonder about our priorities in life. We pay our entertainers fantastic incomes, and our soldiers live a lifestyle barely above poverty. In vast numbers, we buy specialty coffees, teas and juices, multiple times a day, for a price per cup that would feed the needy in third world countries for a week.

Today is Remembrance Day and what do we remember?

> crows dance,
> pick at roadkill
> heads bow

Holy Days On Sale

Christmas carols and a decorated pine dominate the center of the mall. Weary shoppers sit on benches, bags piled around their feet. Shoulders sag, tired eyes watch the procession of people flow past.

Sale signs poke up above racks of clothing, hang from shelves stocked with wide assortments of goods. People touch, look, move on. Others grab, run to the tills.

> tree decoration –
> a fireplace beckons
> through window snow

Midnight*

In the forest, treetops sway frenetically. The steady hiss of wind gives way only for the deeper swoosh of strong gusts. Broken bits of tree branches litter the path. A fallen tree blocks the way, too heavy to be lifted.

The last day of an old year. A year to be forgotten, a year that will persist in memory. The world rocked – earthquakes, tidal waves, terrorist acts, business failures. Winds of change left their debris.

This first day of a new year, announced by heavy winds, explosions, horns blowing in the streets.

> a cold day
> strangers pass,
> mutter well wishes

* The end of 2011 and the beginning of 2012.

An Inconvenient Life

People get up and leave in the middle of the movie – but I stay. Al Gore shows us charts that illustrate the irrecoverable drowning of our planet, the death of species, the growth of desserts.

I think he's right – and I wonder how I can kill myself. How else can I achieve zero emissions? Given that my body will give off methane emissions, even that act isn't enough.

As I watch the movie, his damning charges trigger deep guilt – and helplessness. I feel both small, too little to make a difference, and too large as a member of the masses. I live, consume non-renewable resources, spew carbon dioxide into a thickening atmosphere, trap heat at the planet's surface. Tons of greenhouse gases. Too much gas for forests and plant life to consume, recycle.

If he can't get masses of people to stop, drop and roll into life saving action, how can I? Sure, I drive less, walk more, take the bus when I can, but this is not enough to prevent us from reaching the trigger point.

a cooper's hawk
twists though the trees
the end of a song bird's song

Moving Backwards

I'm moving back to the place of my birth and 54 years of my life. With substantially increased population, the city has changed dramatically in the ten years that I was away. Sprawling miles beyond the city boundary that I once knew, ring roads now find themselves in the inner city. Traffic volumes and speeds are so high that driving feels like a life threatening event. People, once courteous in a mid size city, are now, in this large metropolis, too focused on their cell phones and their own busy schedules to make room and share the road. What once felt like my tranquil home is now go-go-go, non-stop.

But the trauma of this transition isn't just about the roads. I need to find a new home, a doctor, and a dentist – and all are proving difficult. Professional service providers such as physicians and dentists have patient overloads and aren't welcoming anybody new. Home prices have skyrocketed, and finding a suitable place is pushing me further and further out from the city center. Having abandoned the city years ago, the city is making it difficult for me to return.

This is such a contrast to the place I've just left – a city with an aged population, an easier climate, smaller population size, and much slower pace. I'm in culture shock. I now find this faster pace of life too jarring.

> winter departure
> the geese and swans
> rehearsing their vees

I'll look for a place in the country.

Dead Deer Pass

I'm pretty tense, as usual, wondering what could go wrong. The ground is flat, periodically interrupted by piles of fallen rock – stones as big as your head. This does take a bit of scrambling to climb over the obstructions, but it's easy enough to keep moving forward.

I'm walking in a line of people in this narrow crevice caused by an ancient separation of two massive walls of rock. Shoulder wide, water drips in places along the walls, and light leaks in from the upper surface, fifty feet above our heads. Our leader tells how an ancient geological burp created this huge separation in the rock. We engage in gallows humor as we trudge one hundred and fifty feet through this crevice to get to the other side.

Someone imagines leaping over the gap at the top. Another wonders about the fall – could you slow yourself by reaching out? The largest of our group comments on the narrowing he's noticed as we move forward. The guide assures us that this formation has been stable for thousands of years.

As we emerge onto a shelf of rock overlooking a beautiful canyon, someone asks if we can have lunch.

> deep blue sky
> a deer's skeleton trapped
> in a rock crack

On my iPhone, a beep. News flash – Japan stuck by an earthquake, 8.7 on the Richter scale. The northern portion of Japan has moved 8 feet toward the Pacific Ocean. Major roads have separated in the middle, with one side three feet higher than the other. Buildings designed to withstand a massive earthquake have collapsed. The large cement cooling stacks for nuclear power plants have cracked, leak radiation. Thousands have perished.

> narrow miss with
> his first shot
> a startled rabbit

Big Words

Each day, the dictionary app on my smart phone keeps sending me a new word. Big words I had not known before, such as today's word 'erinaceous – an adjective meaning of the hedgehog kind or family'. I want to learn these words and then someday use them to impress others. I have a growing collection.

Perhaps I could allude to my erinaceous tendency to withdraw and hide behind a prickly personality. Alternatively, I could find a way to describe a woman wearing her rebozo over her head and shoulders, perhaps a coedist of the Advaita school. I could use a reference to e´touffe´e to show that I can write with diacritics; or perhaps describe how the broken heart finagles life's spirit; or call on an eidolon to be the mirror image of my own death's mask.

I might describe a mystical, fenestrated castle in a diabolized wood; put the tragic heroine in the scriptoria, reading her departed lover's note, sibilating her distress. In my own Iliad, a paladin would be sent on an odyssey down the River Styx, encountering my own versions of gorgons, Cyclops, and gigantic cephalopods. Reference to Greek mythology considered de rigueur.

I want to be judged a REAL writer because I've shown an expertise at using words in an efficacious fashion within a moving piece about eschatology, or some other element of the human condition. Oh how I might impress, perhaps even be considered a poet of the highest order.

But would the academics waste time assuming inappropriate symbolism?

> the teacher's arrogance
> a student's understanding
> of the laureate's poem

Okay, this won't work. I don't understand most of the words myself, and they aren't really all that poetic. Plus, my word processor doesn't recognize some of them as properly spelled words.

Carrion Pick At The Future

The gene pool was both cleansed and damaged today. A drunk driver crossed the line, traveling forty over the speed limit, and hit a semi head on. The trucker walked from the wreckage but the Jaws of Life had to be used to extract the deceased from his car. Both his family and a hockey team mourn their loss.

A shooter added to that cleansing by taking his own life, but only after draining from the pool by taking the lives of others. A nation mourns.

What brilliance was dimmed today, what athletic prowess destroyed, what future generations were prevented, what potential leaders taken?

> doe and fawn cross
> the busy road
> a murder of crows

San Diego In The Rear View Mirror

Heavy traffic flows out of this large city, speeding beyond the limit, then slowing to a crawl, then back to speed – repeated each time a new exit appears on this twelve lane divided highway. Our eyes are large with strain to see what is in front, beside and coming at us.

We enjoyed the city but now swear we would hate to live there if this is the traffic one has to survive going into and exiting from this metropolis.

> sunset on ocean waves
> surfers walk their boards
> home

Our Addictions

the new born unit
contented sleep
and bubbles from milky lips

And then, what do we become?

He looks at every woman with sexual assessment, tinges his language with innuendo, constantly searches for the willing, masturbates multiple times a day, dreams of gratification with multiple partners, wakes each day with a burning need.

She craves the taste and sensation every minute, thinks of lunch break as a chance to have a few, visits the bar immediately after work, hides bottles in secret places, remembers her first taste with deep longing, wakes to an urgent need for 'just one'.

Some fill their workday with fantasies about their nights. Getting out to the social scene churns their adrenaline, gives them purpose – looking good, flirtation, hooking up, ecstasy – all part of the ritual. Morning emptiness starts each day.

Some work long days, strive for the income that sets achievers apart, gain the means to buy the lifestyle that other's crave. Some spend just to have, to show off accomplishments, to say they have whatever is the latest and greatest. Early mornings and long drives, lost hours.

I take more than a reasonable helping, hold conflicting cravings, rise only to visit the fridge, convince myself that small snacks won't hurt, go to bed bloated, and have buffet dreams.

emergency room
hustling nurses
and moaning patients

115

The Deferrals We Make

She'll retire the ballet slippers she wore
far too long, as she tiptoed through relationships,
matching her steps to various partners,
wearing costumes too constricting,
acting roles choreographed by others. *

In her poem, Shirley writes of a woman who has tired of all the deferrals she made to sustain relationships with men – perhaps implying 'every woman.'

At a reading of her poem in a mixed group, I bark out, "Its too one sided." I argue that we all defer to some degree to make relationships work. The issue is how much we defer, whom we blame for our choices, and how much we allow ourselves to be aware of the accommodations made by our partners.

I wanted a partner who stood her ground. Influenced by the feminism of her age, she came to assert herself, be more specific about what she wanted, to hold on to more of herself. She insisted that she was no longer going to be one of the disadvantaged women, giving over to the needs of her partner.

And yet, to preserve the relationship, she made concessions – as did I. Unlike Shirley's heroine, instead of ceasing all deferral and accommodation, she chose relationship – which does mean some accommodation, and the tension that comes from those gifts we try to give each other.

> high divorce rate, lost relationships
> beneath so many beds,
> only one pair of slippers

We each retired some of our dreams for something more, danced with care through our relationship, wore constricted ways of being, and yet, in so doing, achieved much more with each other.

* Excerpt from the poem 'Barefoot' by Shirley Serviss

A Pensive Day

The article drew my attention, indicating that suicide rates of men over 65 years of age are growing. It turns out that we are particularly good at it. One in four known attempts are successful.

Experiencing pain and discomfort in simple movements, I can't blame such men for their choice. I don't want to live alone, bored, trapped in a diminished body with a failing brain. This decision should not be so shameful, seen as a further failure.

> today's email
> a wish just for me,
> "Happy Father's Day"

Today's Revolution

Heavy clouds move in, unleash a storm. Lightening flashes, rain beats a loud percussion on the roof. Flashes of light streak through the window as if in a race to escape the dark skies. Three seconds between the flash and boom... close. Hail mixes with heavy raindrops. Flower petals peal to the ground. Small flash floods course through muddy troughs in the soil. Trees lose their grip, uproot, topple.

The Nightly News first shows us the effects of storms in Egypt, Syria – then the devastation here.

momentary silence
a list of the dead
posted on the wall

What Have They Missed?

The book title declares "Unforgettable Places To See Before You Die". Forty places around the world, and I've seen only one.

And yet, the places near to me did not qualify – the turquoise of Lake Edith with its backdrop of Mount Edith Cavell; the crashing waters of Athabasca Falls; the deer, elk, bears, mountain sheep in Jasper National Park; the vast numbers of migrating birds in the spring and fall at Beaver Lake; the moving sand dunes in south Saskatchewan; the flowing grasses of the undulating prairie; automobile sized boulders deposited by glaciers in Red Rock Coulee; the majestic flight of pelicans over Pigeon Lake.

None of these wonders qualify?

> fall colours
> an open map
> on the passenger seat

Wi-Fi Generations

She uses her iPad to play her favorite games, buys new apps on iTunes, and FaceTimes with family and friends. Her iTunes account holds a credit balance in anticipation of her next purchase. She pokes at the screen with confidence and assurance that everything will work as expected.

> 92 years of age
> a gout ridden foot
> rests on a pillow

Hers is loaded with educational apps for children her age. Her iTunes account holds a credit balance in anticipation of her next purchase. After hours of use, she complains about sore and dry eyes and we remind her to periodically stop looking at her screen and blink. She says the games are "so fun."

> 4 years of age
> a settled moment
> before sleep time

Winter Blues

mid December
a blank Christmas
gift list

I've been feeling low lately as my body becomes Santa Claus and my spirit becomes Scrooge. Retired and living a sedentary life, pinching pennies to prolong my savings, I've become quite reclusive, frugal, boring. My interest in the outer world is minimal and I connect only infrequently with family and a few friends through e-mail and text messages. Being alone is okay, generally not the root of my troubles, but the symptom.

Christmas eve
an undecorated tree
in a cardboard box

I've stooped to even lower levels of will power, drive, determination. I've become a piece of broccoli in a long neglected vegetable tray. I've given up pursuit of physical wellbeing, creative endeavor, productive sharing, development of hard earned knowledge, generosity and charitable spirits, all in favor of lethargy.

late December
Christmas eggnog
past its due date

And now it's time to set goals and make New Year's resolutions. Serious change is required.

a chart on the wall
for stars and checkmarks
a new energy policy

Today's Incoming

Living rather reclusively in a rural setting, I open my e-mail in anticipation of a few messages from my friends, find only spam.

The subject line of one is "Winter Photography: Tips for Taking Great Photos in the Cold!" Well, that could be useful to me because I certainly live in a cold weather climate – minus 27 this morning with a heavily frosted windshield.

The subject line of another says "Influencers share their tips for starting a new job" and that could apply to me. I've been retired now for six years and I'm a little rusty when it comes to employment.

A third cries out "Get the most out of your extended warranty." Having lived beyond what I was told at 13 would be my likely life span, I guess I'm into my extended warranty period. I sure would like to get the most out of it.

The last one reads "Obama to Employers: Mandatory Paid Sick Days" and that one excites me. I hope to start a new job soon, taking pictures out in the cold. I'll need both paid sick days and an extended warranty. I'll want to work for a long time so I won't become one of the homeless elderly.

> market correction
> a life's savings
> just got smaller

Lazy Mexicans?

On vacation in Bucerias, Mexico, I'm struck by how hard the locals work.

A man sweeps the cobble stone streets with a wire broom, a pregnant gal carries a tin wash bucket on her head and calls out "Muffins". Vendors travel up and down the beach carrying their wares, some sporting heavy rugs, some cases of silver jewelry, some wearing dozens of hats, little children holding boxes of bubblegum, women carrying reams of clothing in their arms.

In the heat, workmen rip up uneven cobblestones, level the under surface, and re-lay the stones with cement to hold them in place. An old man sits on a street corner weaving multicolored baskets. A mentally handicapped man gets on the bus and walks from passenger to passenger selling suckers for a pittance – the purchase justified as a donation. Divers spend all day in salt water clinging to inner tubes, chopping oysters off rocks from the sea floor. An old woman scrubs a hot griddle beside roadside tables.

Given this contradictory evidence, I wonder where such prejudices come from. What leads to conversations where "those lazy Mexicans" is said with such bitterness.

> dinner time
> the children seen
> but not heard

The Cottage Life

Warm temperatures turn winter's heavy snowfall into drips that collect in puddles on the front deck, pools of water on the road, and ponds on the surface of the thick ice that still covers Pigeon Lake. The blue sky with scudding clouds, is reflected in the pools below the feet of Canadian Geese standing on the ice, turning the world upside down.

Skidoos are now parked at empty cabins producing a welcome silence. The fox that runs through my yard, the squirrel that surfaces from his tunnels in the snow, the many varieties of birds that visit the feeder, all riches to savor.

It hasn't always been this way. I burned myself out working to create a business that ultimately had little soul, little satisfaction. For much of my life, I lived amidst the hustle and bustle of a big city, took few vacations, spent my money and attention on possessions no longer of value.

I now live a peaceful and contemplative life in relative seclusion.

> a purple crocus
> as snow melts,
> dust and dirt also appear

Driven

The announcer yells out a ten-minute warning and cacophony breaks out. Dogs howl, bark, whine, nip at each other, jump in the air as far as their short tethers will allow. Racers put harnesses on their restless dogs. Multiple hands hold the harnessed dogs until the team is fully attached to the sled, walk the dogs and sled to the start line, hold them back, and dodge and slide as the dogs jump as if to pull away, bark to get going, and howl to complain that the sled isn't moving.

The starter counts down the minute to the race's start. 60, 30, 15, 10, 9, 8, 7, 6. He raises his arm in front of the sled and his five fingered hand comes out as he says 5, then 4, 3, 2, 1 with his last finger extended, drops his arm and the sled is free to go. The dogs jump up and forward, back legs digging in, chest straining against the harness, and the sled moves. As the team coordinates, the sled gains momentum and they're off.

> a log fire burns
> in a huge steel wheel
> warm thoughts

I snap pictures of all of this, trying to capture the wonder. Everything fascinates me because it's a new experience. Not as excited as the dogs but close, I'm learning what I can by talking with racers and volunteers, trying to understand what compels these people to own so many dogs, to travel so far to race them, and to do the work that a race set-up and take down requires.

Then I remember my own youthful obsession.

> river rapids
> kayaks and gear loaded
> on the roof of the van

A Turbulent Planet

In the past few weeks, middle earth has erupted with several deadly earthquakes in other parts of the globe.

Today, I'm standing in the crater that is Yellowstone National Park, taking pictures of steam rising from thermal vents, of deadened terrain where life is stifled by sulfurous gases, of geysers spewing water and steam high in the air. Momentarily quiet vents suddenly spit hot water and soil.

Unconcerned bison walk across barren surfaces littered with fallen trees, marked with warning signs that declare the thin crust can break through at any moment and cause severe burning. Layers of minerals build up around the vents, taking on wondrous colors and patterns.

I've already been advised that the crater surface sits above two massive magma pools and that the underworld is anything but settled. Here, the cycle of venting and bubbling continues as I move about the park looking for the next photo opportunity.

> deep azure pools,
> red, orange, yellow rings
> news of the number
> of dead and missing
> in turbulence elsewhere

The Challenge

"I have a test for all of you" he says.

The three of us turn to hear the challenge. Four friends, we're in Canyonlands National Park, hiking and shooting photographs of this unusual terrain. We wonder what he is about to ask of us.

"See that tree over there", pointing at a small gnarly dwarf perched on a rounded rock ledge and leaning severely to the right. "That's my favourite tree. I'm still waiting for someone to take a picture that truly captures its essence. See what you can do."

Each of us studies this subject, wondering what makes it a favourite tree in this land of scrub, dessert sand, white and red rock formations, with many stunted trees scattered throughout. Why this particular tree?

Yes the dry, weathered and wrinkled bark gives the tree character, but this could be said for most of the trees. Size isn't atypical – the lack of water, frequent wind, hot dry air makes it very tough for trees to grow here. It leans, but so do most of them. It seems to grow in the barest of soil, persisting in the harshest of circumstances with little nutrients available to support life; but all the trees on the upper plains and ridges seem to grow as if miracles. This tree sits alone on top of a smooth ledge of white rock. Is that it – a solitary survivor reminding him of the hardness of life, the very aloneness of being?

We each scramble over the rock, circle this tree, quite possibly having similar thoughts – is he just putting us on, picking a tree at random, a tree like any other; or is there something special about this particular tree?

> "the best report card ever"
> the young boy
> cuddles his puppy

Aging

Now sixty-nine years of age, I'm a participating member of the baby boom. As a collective, we grow increasingly conscious of the diminishing capacities of our mind and body; shift our daily awareness to our own mortality; and for some, focus on more spiritual concerns than we did as youngsters. We no longer just assume we will be around when the sun rises tomorrow. These haibun show you something of how I experience and how I am dealing with my own aging and mortality.

What's My Legacy?

The twisted arbutus tree leans precariously, sheds its skin in rolls – like papyrus scrolls bearing ancient writings as a legacy to the future.

I wonder: What wisdom, what accomplishments am I leaving as my own legacy? Certainly a bit of an inheritance, but something of what I learned in life might be a more significant gift to my children. I've lived a full life, accomplished a lot. I should have something to share. Is this the habit of all men who pass this late season – to think about what they could pass on to others? Earned wisdom perhaps?

Thoughts like "I wish I'd invested as much in my family as I invested in my work"; or "I wish I hadn't let so many fears direct my life's choices"; or "Our relationships need to be nurtured everyday with joy, love, forgiveness, sharing time together" or "Don't be afraid to give full body hugs." But I don't wish to just deliver what others have already said.

As I search for my own unique voice, I have little more to offer than, "Peanut butter goes well with cheese, but too much can cause great discomfort."

> empty nest –
> the coopers fledged
> and left

Crossing Paths

With the van tightly packed, I take final leave of this city where I grew up, raised my family and started a business.

I wanted to stay, to solve the problems of a failing company, to finish on a high. Instead, I move from disappointment into retirement at too early an age.

As I drive on in the rain, thoughts drift and feelings move through me like the songs on my CD player.

Suddenly a wet and bedraggled bear cub dashes on to the road, stops right in front of me.

I skid to a stop. The bear and I take a few moments to stare at each other. In my mind, I become this creature – lonely, hungry, lost and startled. Like the bear, I wasn't paying attention and wound up where I am.

> sun-dried road –
> slug trails reflect
> the morning light

Battle Scars

The invisible gash up my forearm burns. My back aches from crashing into a wall. A buttock feels the pain from too many lunges. Each turn and twist is agony between my ribs and below my right shoulder blade. My dry throat croaks from too many curses, shouts of self-inspiration, and sighs pleading to the gods – "Please give me air".

Unfortunately, this aftermath of yesterday's racquetball game is too much for any over-the-counter pain reliever.

> a black bird
> in the talons of a kestrel
> cries for life

Meaningful Life

late fall
still rich green vines
climb the trees

Heavy drops left over from the night rain fall from tree branches, provide the only sound. The air is full of the smell of humus as the fallen leaves rot, merge with moist dirt on the forest floor. And then a surprise – the sound of a solitary bee moving through the forest.

I compare my lazy walk with the industriousness of this creature's flight. Recently retired, I haven't yet come to terms with how I spend my time. Old voices echo in my mind,

"A man must work hard for a living, go to work early, come home late."

"He should go to bed exhausted."

"A real man must pursue a better life for his family."

Now that I don't live that life, I have jarring arguments with myself. I mull over what I'm becoming – useless, or finally getting in touch with the here and now; lost, or just accepting; finding moments of peace, or cocooning in fear; a student of a meaningful life, or just a failure.

late fall
a grey squirrel
chases back and forth

Season of Decay

bright sunlight
after grey skies
rotting leaves

Several months after a forced early retirement, I feel both empty, without purpose, and curious about living in the moment.

I look at job ads and find moments of excitement as I imagine myself in those that match my skills. However, such fantasies are quickly replaced by an inertia – a resistance to going back to work, a reluctance to start all over again, and even a hopelessness because previous applications have been ignored.

Is it avoidance when I would rather take time to enjoy the sun, to write about the moment, to take photographs of things not previously noticed; or, is it coming to my senses?

children's laughter
deep in the forest
– remembering

After Retiring

        a calm evening
        the snoring
        of a contented sleeper

Six months after retirement, I now notice what actually grows and lives in a nearby forest, the beautiful blossoms of flowers in the neighbors' yards, bees swarming lavender, worms emerging after a rain, dew soaked spider webs strung from tree to tree.

I do things that I enjoy – writing, taking pictures, editing them, hiking in new areas with my canine companion, developing a web page to share what I produce.

Recollections of going to work have faded, as I rise with hope for the wonder of each new day.

        a new day
        his digital camera
        captures the Kodak moment

The Way We Were

I miss the old courtesies. Drivers would stop, let you join the flow of traffic. Doors would be opened. Places in line would be protected. Seats on buses relinquished to others with a greater need. Forgotten wallets would be returned, personal property honoured. People were more respectful of each other, more careful to prevent injury, embarrassment or discomfort.

I miss such innocence. I wish for a return to that time of my youth – a time with so little possessions, nothing much to lose, a period of being simply open-ended, a community around me that meant no harm.

> old man's slippers
> a floppy fit
> and many scuff marks

Fifty-Nine Today

Remembering the cake my mother made for me when I was eight, I called her last night and got her recipe. Today, I follow her instructions, immersed in fond memories. I salivate over fantasies of a heavy, moist, white cake with butter icing like only she could make.

> ingredients
> arranged on the counter
> a warming oven

I cream butter, sift cake flower with baking soda and salt, add milk, vanilla, and vinegar. The mixer hums, the bowl turns. I use the spatula to steer the mix toward the spinning blades, closely monitor the texture of the mix… and reflect on this past year.

> a surplus of time
> an old man
> reflects on his age

My first year of retirement has been interesting. In the early stage, depression hit me as I found myself bereft of purpose and without a structure to my day. In the middle of the year, this slough of despond slowly turned to calm, a respite from the many travails that led to being adrift.

> the fine script
> of her old recipe
> remembered birthdays

In the oven, the cake takes shape, rises, gradually takes on a gold luster. As the aroma fills my kitchen, I remember a simple time when a boy looked forward with great anticipation, feel the same excitement today.

> the song recedes –
> ice cream melts
> on the still warm cake

Returning

      a chickadee flits
      from branch to branch
      changing weather

I reluctantly walk my dog. Minus 21 degrees, my breath fogs the air, leaves frost on my glasses. The dog, in winter boots, stops, looks at me as if to say, "What are we doing here?"

I lived the past nine years on Vancouver Island, without snow, above zero temperatures, no heavy winter clothing… and with flowers that bloom in the winter. That softer life stole my edge, that love I used to have for living in Northern Canada.

So you might ask, "What am I doing here?"

I've come to be with my granddaughter, to watch her learn to crawl, to hear her first words, to let her know me as her grandfather.

      unpacked boxes
      stacked on the floor
      an old man's home

I've made the better choice.

Little Gifts

       on the lawn
       pileated woodpeckers
       and their chick

She lies on my chest, breathing quickly as she settles from her meal, fussing a bit as she adjusts her arms and legs to get comfortable. Her rust colored hair, new born smell, little squeaks as she processes the fluids she has just taken.

I wonder how I missed this with my own children when they were infants forty years ago … or has memory just escaped me. Work, the financial pressures of too little income for a young family, and the demands of an intensive school program are easier to recall than the bliss of being with my own children in the first days of their lives.

As a grandparent, this is a new luxury – nothing else matters right now.

       fall colours
       soft pink skin
       on a soft pink blanket

No Sale Yet

I've come to visit a house that sits empty, waiting for a buyer. These empty rooms, this empty spirit, no longer filled with hopes and dreams. Dust rests on counter tops. Echoes of my breathing come back to me like memories of the life that I lived here.

Anticipations of a quick sale have realized only disappointment. It seems the market has shifted its interest to property of a different type. My only recourse is to drop the price, hope that someone will come to appreciate what I liked about this place.

> closing edge of winter
> song birds sing
> but not yet in spring colors

I wish to relocate, to start a new home a thousand kilometers away. I'm prevented by the lack of money, the desired outcome from the sale of my existing property. I wait impatiently.

> warmer days
> dirty snow recedes,
> reveals new shoots of grass

Waiting

Her 89th birthday approaches. She sits with her legs on a footstool because when she doesn't, water builds up in her ankles and leaks from scratches on her shins. Life is no longer full for this mother of three, grandmother to four and great grandmother to five.

They have busy lives and she sits in her loneliness, working on puzzles, watching British mysteries on TV. She makes her own breakfast of dried toast and a half sandwich for lunch, but calls out to the local shops for delivery of her supper. Her own mother lived to 94 so she firmly believes she has more years left in this life.

> a warm house
> the long running television soap
> in its last season?

She does not talk about what comes next, but I think she holds to a concept of life in heaven after death. I wonder what her heaven might be like – a return to the life of her youth; the piety of angels amongst the clouds; sitting at the side of the man himself; an end to the loneliness surrounded by her own ancestors?

> deep sleep
> dreams of ice cream cones
> and Saturday dances

Prickly Thoughts

Hunters' guns explode in the distance. Dried leaves swish along the road and crows sway in the buffeting wind. At lake's edge, geese and ducks gather in their groups, slowly paddle away as I approach. I'm walking the lakeshore road, deep in contemplation. On this hallows eve, I'm thinking about the coming winter and the mystery of our leaving.

At 92, my father, in the throes of congestive heart failure, chose to forgo medical treatment and tried to will himself to death. His dying was not so easy. During a late night check, a nurse adjusted his sheets. He woke and asked "Have I died yet?" Several nights later a series of deeper breaths was followed by one shallow exhale and he was gone.

My wife was told she had terminal cancer and rapidly descended into frailty. With frequent doses of morphine to alleviate pain, she disappeared into a coma, mouth open, shallow breathing, unresponsive to touch or talk. On her last day, her daughter held her hand, said "It's okay to go Mom. We'll be alright." and she slipped away.

How will I leave this life?

I have no belief in after-life, so no faith will console me. I have so many things I want to do and a chronic feeling that I won't get them done. I cling to them as my purpose in these remaining days I have. Will I resist going into the dark night or will I reach out my arms in an attempt to leave my body for something waiting on the other side.

> a crushed porcupine
> at road's edge
> prickly thoughts

In The Moment

My massage therapist, a beloved friend, frequently told me, "Breath, just be in the moment." Good advice to live by I suppose.

While I walk a country road, I wonder just what exactly is being in my moment?

Is it noticing the clear blue sky, the easy feel of 16 degrees Celsius on the skin, the fall colors on the trees, the sound of the ducks and geese out on the lake, the flight of a chickadee as it darts in front of me? Or is it feeling the burn of esophageal reflux, the congestion in my chest, the phlegm that irritates my throat, the pressure within my eyes, the soreness of an injured ankle, the feeling of high blood pressure that accompanies a generalized anxiety, the shortness of breath while I walk a hilly country road?

I wonder what's in my massage therapist's moment right now. Early this week, she had a brain tumor the size of a tennis ball removed. She has to sit at home for post surgery recovery, wait for the pathology report. Is she able to remind herself to breath?

Can I?

> gusts
> yellowing leaves
> flutter

Anxious Meditation

I sit to meditate for the first time in many years, focus on my breath to initiate relaxation. In surprise, I experience a quickness of breath – then realize I'm anxious. Although this meditation is supposed to involve focus on breath, my thoughts drift, ask, "About what?" and answer, "There's too little time left."

Thoughts on a tangent, focus on breath, thoughts on a tangent, focus on breath… "What's so important for me to do?"

I have a growing relationship with a young granddaughter and hope to see her into her adult years before it's my time to go. I've recently started writing several books – so that I don't finish with the feeling that all I've done has been wasted. I also have travels I want to do.

I bought a motor home so I could see more of North America, and have only briefly visited familiar spots in B.C. and Alberta. I want to hear wheels on pavement and swim in strange lakes. I want to travel more of the world – Portugal, India, China, Japan, New Zealand.

Renovations to my recently purchased house have to be completed. I have a bookcase full of unread books and an extremely comfortable easy chair. There are dishes to cook for the first time. I've new breaths to take.

> many colored leaves
> fall to the ground
> still Indian summer

Such a Welcome

With her hair freshly done at the beauty parlor, she smiles brightly when she greets me. Enjoying life at this moment, she has forgotten how she wished for death just two weeks ago, when terribly ill from what appears to have been a drug reaction.

Today, she has energy, and choses to ignore tomorrow's pending lumpectomy, particularly risky at her age of 90. The cancer is stage 2 so might not even turn out to be the cause of her death, but they've decided to remove the lump. The surgery itself is a risk, and she'll feel rotten afterwards. Will she welcome death then?

> this sunny day
> her night clothes
> laid out on the bed

Good Versus Evil

early spring
the once hibernating bear
emerges from his cave

During the day, he's a good boy. He eats reasonably, exercises both body and mind, engages in physical workouts and mindful activities. He greets people with courtesy and respect, concerns himself with learning, writing and visual creativity.

harsh fall
a squirrel frequently
visits the feeder

At night, he becomes an evil old man, intermittently sedentary or walking to the fridge to find the most inappropriate evening snack. Remote in hand, he surfs the channel guide, flips from show to show, unable to settle on one thing, concentrating only on the next craving.

old mule
a hard pull
on the fraying harness

Averages

When I was a kid, the average life expectancy of men my father's age was 65, and of women 72. Both my parents lived into their nineties, and my mother at 91, is still going strong. Improvements in diet, lifestyle, and medical treatments have all contributed to an extension of the expected average lifespan of most North Americans.

At 67, I'm wondering how long men my age are now expected to live. If we experience as significant a gain as my parents did, does this mean that I could make it beyond 100 years of age? If so, what will I do with all that time?

> warm morning
> multi-coloured leaves
> still linger

Differences

At 67, I step off the porch, high step through the snow, shudder at the wet cold around my ankles, and grimace when my fingers touch the cold handle of the car door.

At 3, she laughs, runs down the steps, drags her feet to create channels in the snow, throws handfuls in the air, and sticks out her tongue to catch the flakes.

> a heavy scarf
> feathered angel wings
> on a child's body

> large flakes
> a battered old hat
> and thick warm gloves

Aging and The After Effects of Exercise

Half grown ducklings separate themselves more and more from their parents as they explore the rather large beaver pond, but race to mother's side when any form of danger appears. When alarmed, they practically run across the scum, quacking their angst.

I move much more slowly in the midst of my own discomfort. A tight band of tension circles my waist, inhibits my steps, causes grimaces as I advance. My exclamations are grunts of pain, but there is no mother to run to.

> an old barn
> timbers creak
> under the weight

Shrinkage

My peak of 5'11 7/8" (I used to say 6 feet) is now 5'10". A once lofty self-esteem is now in the dirt. Where reflections of a white knight shone from a daughter's eyes, now I see only another worry in a busy life. A wife's excitement has been replaced by yawns of boredom. Perfectly tailored suits have been replaced by cottons and khakis that sag like wet laundry on a clothesline. An old public reputation has turned into reclusion. Boxes of once proud work gather dust in the basement. Mountains of hope, expectations and plans now just junk to be discarded.

I consider the thief, cry out… "Give it back!"

A whisper returns …"You invited the taking, so I took."

> this cold winter
> birds peck
> at drooping sunflowers

> heat waves
> spring rains now
> just puddles of mud

Bedtime Reading

An analysis of studies* found that when people walk just 174 minutes a week, they have a 19% reduced risk of death, compared to the most sedentary people.

Incredible. If I walk three hours a day for just five days a week, I won't die. You do the math. 103%. It works.

And don't forget the benefits of seven days a week. 138%. Not only immortal but I'll walk with the gods.

"Now I lay myself to sleep..." Isn't there some prayer that starts like that and finishes with a hope I wake in the morning? Here's hoping.

> old man
> this long wait
> for spring to come

* Mandy Oaklander, Time.com, January 22, 2015

The Big Event

It's that annual time of year when I get a physical exam from my doctor. The nurse weighs me, measures my height, and takes my blood pressure. The tightness of the cuff hurts and I notice she writes down 142 over 85. She tells me my pulse is 72, to take off all clothes except my underwear, and leaves.

He arrives, asks how I'm doing and proceeds to discount many of my complaints, disabuse me of any concerns about my various skin tags and a changing growth on my back, tells me that getting winded when I climb hills is just because I'm out of shape. He asks if I get any exercise and I tell him about my fifty-minute walk almost every day. He gives a curt "GOOD" in response.

He gets me up on his table, checks my blood pressure again. Says its normal this time. He puts a stethoscope to my back and chest, asks me to breath heavily. I sound like a stalker on the telephone. He says "Yup. Out of condition." He pokes and prods my gut, asks if I've been doing okay. I tell him I had a gall bladder attack on Christmas eve from eating greasy pork ribs. He tells me I could have surgery or chose to eat more carefully.

I'm told to turn on my side. He pushes my knees up toward my chest, tugs down my under pants. I feel the cold of the lubricant and the stretch of his rubber glove as he utters a sorry. He says, "We're done. Get dressed. I'll be back with a requisition for lab tests."

different pokes
an afternoon quickie
with a sympathetic wife

Life's Septembers

*"Should a man reach 80, he has only 80 Septembers. It does not seem like many said that way. It seems as if there had been so few, each one should have been better used." ***

My own 69 Septembers were spent without paying much attention, especially as I aged. In childhood, fullness was found in the last rays of summer, the excitement of back to school, the start of street hockey. As a young teen, time was filled with books from the library, music on a transistor radio, and fantasies of becoming something great. Late adolescence was focused on the opposite gender, the green of the gridiron, staying out of trouble at school.

Then the Septembers of marriage, raising children, pursuit of career success, and dealing with responsibilities all pushed awareness out of the moment and into worries about the future. Retirement gives more time to be in the present, but regret about missed opportunities pulls awareness into the past.

> last day of summer
> a tired old man
> budgets for the future

* John D MacDonald, The Scarlet Ruse

Embers To Ash

Companions for forty years, the three of us ride our bikes over mountain trails, watchful for bears, warning them off with bike bells. The days are hot, the ground is hard and dry, wildlife seems to have moved deeper into the cooler woods, unavailable for us to see.

This year something feels different. Each of us has experienced changes that come with our aging.

> deep conversations
> into the night
> fire embers glow

Laying in bed, I feel aches in my joints, a dull throb in my back, the soreness from sitting too long on a bike seat, and think of my pending birthday, of our relationships that pull us in different directions, of how little time we have together.

Overnight, a forest fire erupts from a lightning strike. Smoke fills the sky, cuts our time short, forces us to take to the road. We hug, go our separate ways.

> the forest burns
> will there be a bumper crop
> of morels next year

Good Times

I've just returned from a trip to Jasper National Park with two forty-year companions who know the worst and the best of me. We rode bikes, enjoyed the cuisine at Jasper Park Lodge while sitting at tables overlooking Lac Beauvert, and shared evening walks on trails along the Athabasca River.

> deep waters
> how precious the sound
> of wind in ancient trees

> discussing the next
> stage in our journeys
> the golden leaves of fall

Eye Damage

Rough housing in the pool with my granddaughter, I was flipping her over and throwing her into the deeper water. We were having a great time.

Noticing an unexplained piece of seaweed in the water, I reached out to pull it from the pool. It shifted just out of reach. Then I noticed that it moved as I moved my point of focus. I also detected some white flashes in my peripheral vision as if lightning was flashing off to my side. I didn't know what was happening but knew it had to do with a change in my right eye.

A visit to an optometrist the next morning led to better understanding. A bit of the vitreous fluid in my eye hardened with age, and then just pulled away from the retina. He examined me closely, looking for a retinal tear or evidence of a detached retina. Finding none, he gave me reassuring comments that this was a normal occurrence as we aged, and that my brain would adjust and stop seeing the "floater" that I was calling seaweed. It wouldn't really go away but would no longer be noticeable.

Dependent on my vision for living the lifestyle I live, spending so much time in front of so many screens (my computer, my iPad, my iPhone, TV), I'm not mollified. My sleep is disturbed and I wake with more eye strain, more worries.

> fall temperatures
> with paw elevated, a coyote
> limps across the field

Exciting Sounds

A friend, after first use of his new hearing aids, recently wrote,

> *"I hear more conversations when amongst the mumblers, who are fruitful and have multiplied into plenitudes. I hear the TV with clarity, hear a mosquito buzzing from roughly one province away....."*

I've noticed that I don't hear dialogue well when watching TV, have to ask my spouse to repeat her comments, can't hear what people are saying to me in social situations because of all the white noise from other conversations around the room. My hearing capabilities have diminished with age.

In general, I've noticed that too many people with hearing aids often choose not to use them; so it was good for me to read his enthusiasm for his newfound ability to hear.

I figure maybe there are some upsides:

- my friends might appreciate that I respond when asked to pass the salt;

- my dog might like that I no longer yell at him just to greet him in the morning;

- my partner would no longer feel silly when she whispers sweet endearments in my ear and I mumble back that I also liked the sushi;

- the birds in my yard would no longer have to strain to raise the volume of their song so that I put food in the feeder;

- I could hear what's being said when I talk to myself in public places, shift to a whisper instead of a shout;

- I could hear the sizzle of burning bacon in the fry pan in the mornings, and get up on time;

- my throat would be less sore from no longer saying, "What?"

- I could actually get to have ice cream when my spouse very quietly asks from the kitchen, "Would you like some too?"

- my friends would actually talk to me and not everyone else when they want to be heard.

I'm sure there are also some downsides, but I can only think of the increased ability to hear my own body noises; and the noise from constant genital scratching would probably be irritating.

> today, a dead bat
> below the window
> no hearing aids yet

Soixante-Neuf

My sixty ninth birthday. I can't get the playful meaning of the French phrase out of my head, so I guess I still have the joy of life.

My spouse prepared a triple layer white cake with creamy buttermilk icing and blueberry jam between the layers. It's huge.

> her wide grin
> meets me at the door
> time to eat

Like a record, my mind keeps running the phrase, "you can't have your cake and eat it to" but I'm eating, enjoying and anticipating the leftovers.

Grieving

I have experienced the loss of significant others, and along with these losses, grief. Every so often, that grief rises into my consciousness and I write about it. These haibun show you something of that grief – only something because I tend to sublimate through denial. I share a bit of what has surfaced.

Last Appointment*

The vet gently strokes, prods, takes his temperature, speaks endearments, listens to our description of the latest symptoms.

"His liver and kidneys have shut down completely. I'm sorry but you've got a tough choice to make." A syringe appears.

> a chrysalis stirs
> he leaves
> the room

Old Predictions Come Painfully True

At work, I see the caller ID, answer the phone with a hearty "hello".

Silence then a sobbing, "I'm sorry." I don't know what she is sorry about, wait for more as she collects herself. "I have cancer. There is a large tumor in my lung."

Instantly, disorganized thoughts flood into my mind. She had a medical nine months ago and her x-rays were clear. How can that be? More fragile lately, we assumed her lupus was acting up. Forty-three years ago we fought about her smoking. I anxiously predicted the smoking would kill her, urged her to quit. To avoid that tension, we found a resolve of sorts. She agreed to smoke outside the house. I agreed to stop nagging. During our camping trip over the past weekend, she was lost in thought, very quiet. She must have suspected.

"I'll be home immediately. Hang in there. We can talk."

> his paw on her knee
> and a gentle stare
> our dog knows

> the predicted tornado
> touched down
> a community devastated

Mona Lisa's Secret

With a half smile, forced – given what she knows, she ponders how she'll tell him. She has many secrets really, but this one must be shared. One hand rests over the other, calms the shaking, holds her in. Afraid of the coming pain, afraid of the leaving that will come, she wets her lips, looks directly into his eyes, deeply sobs, says the words that still haunt, "I'm so sorry. It can't be treated. I'm dying."

> rot in the core
> of the old tree
> won't be long now

Late Arrival

With a choked sob, she accepts the news. Her daughter is pregnant – a long standing wish granted. But the baby will arrive only after her departure. From her sick bed, she croaks, "I was supposed to be there to support her."

    winter night
    the heavy covers
    insufficient

New Visitor In The House

busy doctor's office
a cautious glance
at lung cancer pamphlets

The tumor in her lung actually causes the lung to shrink. The resulting space created in the lung cavity fills with fluid – partially water and partially blood. A great deal of pain is created as the fluid builds, drains downward, stretches the lung cavity and presses on other organs. The first time this fluid was drained resulted in 2 liters of fluid and tremendous relief. Two weeks later, the fluid has returned – and the agony with it. We're told to expect the end soon.

bags full of food
for thanksgiving dinner
the milk container heavier today

The hospice nurse comes at 4:00 a.m. to check on the pain. A large black container is opened, revealing an extensive collection of opiates. The dose is increased and she slides with relief into sleep. Shallow breaths, intermittent deep exhalations, moans that seem to say "No!" Her family sits with her in vigil.

several deer
mill about the yard
as she leaves, a full moon

The Last Cleansing

Learning of her illness was a shock to both of us, but not as much as being told she only had a short time to live. Radiation was suggested to reduce the size of the tumor, to make her more comfortable in her last days. Somehow, we heard this as giving us more time.

Talk about anything that reminds her about dying is very upsetting to her, so we avoid this. We live each day as if she's recovering. There are many things that we could share before she leaves, but don't.

> two strangers
> at the river's edge
> water under the bridge

We could tell each other about the best memories we have of our life together. We could talk about how we enriched each other's lives, how grateful we are to have been together for 43 years, how satisfied we feel about the children that are the fruit of our relationship.

And yes, we could even talk about what has been true between us and what has been lies – to come clean before we part.

But we don't.

> her best friend
> washes her body
> last rites

Her Presence

I periodically catch myself speaking of her in the present tense; saving a TV program I think she would like to watch; worrying about her criticism of something I have done; wanting to share a special moment. Reflections of light on the edge of my glasses, I momentarily think she is nearby.

> half empty house
> our dog waits
> by the front door

> quick movement
> at the corner of my eye
> a mouse or ....

Empty Skies

As we approach, little birds flit amongst the semi-bare branches of the low bush. A large grey squirrel sees the dog, dashes across the path, climbs a tree, peers one eye carefully around the trunk. My dog chafes at his leash. A large gold and orange maple leaf falls from the heights of the tree, clicking through the branches until it joins brethren on the footpath.

Watching the leaf fall, my thoughts turn to my fallen wife. If her beliefs are true, she has joined her ancestors amongst the stars. If my beliefs are true, she's just gone, her light gone with her. Somehow, it would be better to hold her beliefs but I just don't have that faith.

> night falls
> worms till the soil
> and re-cycle waste

Hers

I was just a welcome guest. Now this house is mine alone.

> her electric toothbrush
> unplugged
> silence in the house

I miss the weirdest things. Mostly, right now, I miss those behaviors of hers that used to annoy me – the pleasure she took when smoking, talking to me while I'm listening to others, repetitively stroking me with a touch that was barely there, contradicting me when I was wrong, hiding the kitchen utensils in unpredictable cupboards.

Don't get me wrong, I do miss many good things, but to think of them now, just rips me up. Soon I suspect, I will miss her body and the comfortable ways we developed over 43 years – our sex never lost its excitement. I will miss her presence in the room, the sound of her voice, her laughter, the light snore of her breathing at night, the clothes hanging on the chair by the bed. She warmed this home with well chosen furniture, art work, seasonal flowers, stories of her day, good meals – soon I will allow myself to replace the numbness I feel, with the rage of missing these things. But I'm not ready to fill her house with this just now.

> the logger looks
> at the girth of the tree
> silence in the forest

Unexpected Opening

Almost nine months after my wife's death, I'm at a funeral of a family friend. I've just come to show support.

> her coffin
> conversational murmurs
> as the congregation waits

Upon sitting in my assigned pew, I read the handout describing the life of the deceased, and tears erupt from my right eye. I can't explain why the left eye remains dry, or why this brings out such intense feelings of missing MegAnne. Every day, I have pangs of sadness but this is much more.

> heavy rain
> water gushes to the road
> in a single channel

All through the service, I mentally flip to my own memories of MegAnne. Tears flow freely, my skin flushes hot, my body shrivels into itself, grief reaches up and grabs me by the throat, all while I appreciate every word said about the recently departed.

> her eulogy
> mirrors on opposite walls
> stare into infinity

I retreat to my own solitude, feel the warmth of having released buried feelings.

> summer heat
> the old dog sleeps
> at my feet

My Own Memories of Her

Friends stay in touch – ask how I'm doing, wish me well, suggest we get together. Although grateful for their caring, I just want to be alone, not sure if this is the grieving process, or just my avoidance.

When we get together, they share memories of her, try to get me to talk about how I feel. Mostly numb, I don't know what I feel, but know the agitation that surfaces when they ask. I can't sit still, want to run.

It's not that I don't remember. I do – all the time. I'm reminded about her in everything around me. It's just that being reminded by others crowds into the privacy of my own remembering.

> invitation to hospice counseling
> in the dark, under the porch
> a sick dog

Guilty!

Recently asked by a close friend if I feel guilty, I answered too quickly that I do. Later upon reflection, I had to come to a more complete answer.

- Guilty! I survived. She did not.

- Prone to see the negative, I missed many opportunities for play, laughter, and joy.

- Reserving most of my feelings to myself, I was too hesitant to talk about love, to be tender and loving, holding back my touch instead of reaching out to my wife.

- Worrying about what will come of my life now that I'm on my own.

- Not wanting to be alone, quickly turning to another for companionship.

The answer is "Yes". I feel guilt about being the schmuck that I am.

> paw caught in a trap
> decaying leaves
> on the forest floor

And now, there is the guilty pleasure derived from grieving. In the beginning, just numb, I didn't know what was going on inside of me. Only recently, I allow memories and feelings to emerge.

> an old journal
> poems about love
> and living

> noises at the door
> the dog rises, barks
> and wags his tail

Hallowe'en

In his mid 70s, he now speaks Hollywood lumberjack, wears Kevlar pants, and carries two chain saws like a Wild West gunslinger. He's in love for the first time in a long time, writes about late-in-life romance, and no longer talks about deliberate death at 75. It turns out that he has revised that conversation to "when I'm no longer able", smiles more, cracks jokes, laughs, says he's enjoying life more.

At 68, my costume is a threadbare robe, a tattered t-shirt, fraying short pants, and moccasin slippers with broken and stretched threads that allow the nylon sole to flap as I walk. I sit in my den, read about the strangeness of dying, make plans to visit my wife's gravesite, and feel the torment of empty spaces.

> fall meditations
> fog covers
> the nearby waves

Traveling Companions

On this trip, previously planned as an adventure to be taken with a now dead spouse, I'm traveling with another woman. She is a long time friend who shares an interest in photography and the excitement of seeing new places. We travel in my motor home – a large vehicle but a small living space.

Disgusted with myself, I find myself critical of her navigating, how she attends to her tea when we need to be packing up and getting ready to move to our next destination, what she buys for groceries, how she prepares the food.

I'm reminded of a history of bickering with my wife – the way that I found fault with her navigating; her slow pace and reluctance when leaving old places for new; how she made her choices when shopping; the way that she cooked.

I regret getting lost in criticism, my failure to clearly let her know how much she mattered to me.

> card shop
> "Wish you were
> here"

In turn, I'm also aware now of my failure to clearly let my traveling companion know how much she matters to me.

Close

For much of ten years we were very close. In the last six of those years, a day seldom went by where we didn't spend time together. We moseyed through forests, parks, nearby neighborhoods. He had his favorite places and I had mine.

We had our own invented games that we played for hours. Him – more athletic, more capable. Me – more inventive, the encourager, usually the watcher.

Most observers would have looked at us and thought that I was the responsible one, taking charge, looking after his needs.

However, he was the one that kept me alive, somewhat healthier for the exercise he demanded, and more focused on the here and now. He'd insist on getting out of the house and persist till we did. He'd protect me from strangers, and alert me if anyone approached our home.

He sat with me in my moments of deepest grief, not asking anything of me but just being present. Not afraid to show affection, he would approach and reach out to assure me that I was in his thoughts.

And today, one year later, he is in mine.

> ashes in a box
> well chewed toys
> still piled on his bed

A New Year's Grievance

> noisy night
> an extra place setting
> at the table

She appeared in my fevered dreams last night. I could see her as I often remember her, watching, evaluating, showing disappointment. I've either let her down again, or fulfilled her low expectations.

It's a sad way to re-experience her presence, but I'll take it. She had the ability to remind me that I could be better, so perhaps I've made this part of her, a part of me. For whatever reason, she's welcome. I've missed her.

> anniversary wish
> a tear rolls
> down a cheek

Overweight, lethargic, avoiding completion of various projects, I set some enthusiastic goals for the year. I so wanted to get off to a good strong start. Instead, yesterday was another day of doing nothing.

> fresh snow
> blocks the roadway
> her voicemail message

Just a Moment

In the closet, the line-up of her jackets presents the range of colors that she wore – purples, browns, beiges, some muted blues. In silence, they march along the rack, taking my memory to her.

Her gentle presence, quiet voice, respectful attention to anyone present, remind me that I too should gentle, slow my thoughts, pay attention.

> a single bird call
> from the forest
> an overcast day

It Ain't Easy

The tenth day, I'm sitting vigil waiting for his last breath.

Dying is proving much harder than he expected. Congestive heart failure brought him to the hospital. A racing heart, shallow breathing, lungs full of fluid, disorientation, low energy tie him to the bed.

He speaks clearly to anyone who will listen – he wants to die. He's had ninety good years. He's bored, constantly experiences pain, has nothing but more to look forward to, doesn't want to be saved. He asks them to "pull the trigger" but they won't. Opiates are provided to increase his comfort but not to lead the way.

Each time he wakes, he expresses disappointment over still being here. One morning, he expresses his anger at himself because he ate some little thing from his breakfast tray. He doesn't understand why he did such a thing when he doesn't want to live, just as he doesn't understand why he can't will himself to death. Every few hours, he jerks upright, shocked that he is still here.

Now, he lays without stirring, larger spaces between each breath, eyes glassed over, a crackle in his lungs as the fluid reduces the space for air to enter. As the time between exhalations grows longer and the crackle is louder, I sit and wonder if each one will be his last.

At 5:30 in the morning, his death rattle then silence.

> dark room
> the rise of the bed sheets
> continues in my mind

Momentary Silence

There is no reply. There never is. I'm talking to her picture on the fireplace mantel. She's been gone almost four years; but I see her smile, smell her hair, measure her body against mine. I more than miss her – I ache for her! And without any real faith in an afterlife, I ache to know she's all right.

> dripping gutters
> leaf tea leaches
> into the parched soil

Shared Celebrations

It's the 47th anniversary of our marriage. We shared a double wedding with my wife's sister and husband, so I send them well wishes. They'll be going for a nice dinner to celebrate, as they've done over the years. For many of them, we were there.

At these dinners, we would reminisce about that day, our nervousness, excitement, tiredness after all the planning and work leading up to the big event. Someone would be sure to mention how upset I got when the drunk cousins abducted my new bride at the reception, how awesome the grand cathedral was as a choice, how many people attended – almost always leading to the question, "Who's still alive?"

> falling leaves
> the image of her
> gravesite in my mind

The Fifth Anniversary

Following a long drive from Edmonton to Victoria in a severe snow storm, I'm here, clearly intending to visit her, yet I don't know what to say.

I stand at her gravesite with her best friend and her sister. They comment on the health of the Western Cedar that draws nutrients from her decomposition*, put voice to her favorite chants, remember her being. I stand mute.

I think of the rich legacy of her children, her grandchildren, beings she would take great pride in having made possible. I think about how my own life has changed in her absence. I think about what she has missed. I think of giving her news about her still surviving siblings. The times her friends have said they miss her come to mind.

But I'm unable to talk of these things, not knowing if she is anywhere near and able to hear. Mostly, I hope her spirit has gone on to a better place, not knowing if such a thing as an after-life spirit exists.

I feel the irrelevancy of this earthly place, think of the worms, bugs, and plants she has harbored since leaving us, and wonder if this is all there is.

> a lonely day
> cold outside
> and hot memories inside

* MegAnne chose an organic burial – no chemicals, no coffin, no gravesite markers, only a hemp shroud.

Measure Of A Man

Gossip, as gossip is prone to be, was harsh. He was seen by many as a professor who took advantage of his students, hit on the females, put the males on the hot seat in encounter groups, exploiter of his tenured faculty position, taking only the easy ways to instruction and grading.

What is the real measure of a man? Is it what they say about him or what he does? And whose opinion matters?

At the memorial, his children stood in front of our large group and told us of incredible times at his farm. Clearly he gave them permission to be kids. Skinny dipping in the pond. Driving various vehicles around his 160 acres. Swimming as young children in the rapids of the river that runs along the property. Sleeping under the stars. Unchaperoned junior high and high school graduation parties on his land. Learning to take risks, thrilling in the survival of it all. They talked about how he burst out in song, infectiously drawing them and all of their friends into joy. There they sit in front of our gathering speaking words of wisdom – mature, responsible, loving adults revering this man for his permission to be themselves.

Former students praised his experimentation and risk taking as an educator, thanked him for the permission he gave to test themselves in the doing of their lessons. Former colleagues credited his stretching of boundaries for the shape that teaching could take and encouraging them to experiment, try new things in their own classrooms.

His first wife thanked him for the wonderful children they shared. His current companion told us of his forty-year spiritual quest, his constant reminders to be in the moment, his joy at physical activity, his encouragement to live life totally.

> tombstone
> "here lies
> a good man"

Fiction

Every once in a while when I sit down in front of my keyboard and force myself to type, a fictional haibun emerges. Certainly, the content of these haibun show you something of my subconscious processes and in a few cases, something about the darkness that hides there in. These are made up pieces but in their own way show you something about my intimate affairs of fantasy.

Boundaries

A canopy of fir sways in the blue of the sky. With tight embrace, ivy climbs, circles, ascends to the light. An older tree wears a coat of vines thick as fingers. On the cluttered forest floor, encased tree carcasses give evidence of the results of these relationships.

In her trance, she stares out the window, steaming coffee cup in hand, contemplating the papers that lie in front of her. All she'd wanted was a perfect marriage – two people doing things together, spending time, liking what each other liked, talking about everything – being close.

> in the sandbox, she offers
> to help build his castle
> sand flies

One

Lying in a strange bed in a room not her own, a young child remembers – loud voices, screams, a loud bang, silence, someone sobbing, another explosive bang … and then only the creaky sounds of the house she hears when everyone but her is asleep.

Two bodies on the examiner's tables. Large stitched incisions from gut to sternum to shoulder. Two pieces of paper. Two words printed in black ink on the white parchment. "MURDER. SUICIDE."

> a dappled fawn
> crosses the meadow –
> cautious step… by step

Show Time

Cherry red, shinny chrome, velvet on the seats, passion lights for window trim, the deep purr of 289 cubic inches. His elbow hangs out the window, a single hand on the wheel as the other caresses a greased back ducktail. Cruising slowly down main, he checks out the sidewalk action. The girls look back.

Hot night to be cool. Last chance before shipping out.

> marching orders
> red ants attack
> another hill

Old Times

DJ banter
Elvis sings
"Can't Help Falling …"

A look-a-like Elvis, long black hair, white sequined jacket and pants, guitar slung over his shoulder, stands with the young couple below the vintage 'Welcome to Las Vegas' sign. Groom in a blue tuxedo, bride in a long flowing gown, smiles and laughter, Elvis saying "Thank you, Ma'am. Thank you very much".

an old diary
a life no longer
lived

Never Too Old

Too old to care about appearances, he wears the same old tattered sweater and pants that trail threads at the cuffs. Long ago, she stopped dying her hair, frumps about the house in a loose fitting smock. Their days have routine and familiarity. The radio speaks to them like mice in a corner, but they seldom take note. He works at a crossword puzzle, she has her macramé. Knowing each other well, they share silent conversations throughout the day.

        a dark room
        two people
        breathing hard

How to Answer?

He leans forward, asks "What are you doing with yourself, now that you're retired?" Hearing his tone, she imagines an accusation – whatever she is doing, it better be something significant, something worth doing. She doesn't know how to answer.

What does he want to hear – that she volunteered to help the less fortunate in her community, rushed off to New Orleans to help the victims of Hurricane Katrina, offered her services to agencies that serve the hungry and sick in Africa?

Can she tell him she's spent the past six months recovering? Goes to bed after midnight, rises late, reads the paper, fusses about in her garden, plans trips she hasn't yet taken, simply tries to enjoy each moment of her day.

> another breath
> the sunlight creeps
> across the sill

Forgetting

She stands at the sink, wrings liver spotted hands, gazes out the window, not actually seeing, mumbles, "What am I doing over here?"

> cloudy morning
> the hollow knock-knock-knock
> of a woodpecker

In Pursuit

The photograph lies there, abandoned, taking on the dull yellow of age. A slight rip in one corner, finger prints on the gloss, frequently picked up, stared upon, the picture keeps memories alive.

She died too soon, well before living her dreams. She was to be a teacher of children. Barely more than a child, she was attacked, raped and killed by a stalker. The shame of things done to her body, horrible as they were, does not touch the shame of lost potential. Every child loved her, played with her, opened up to her.

> crocus blossoms
> yesterday,
> winter cold

Unable to anticipate more of this life on his own, knowing she really did love him, he brews a special concoction that only he will drink. Sitting to tea time, satisfied that his actions are correct, he begins his own journey, intending to meet her there.

> under the teacup
> an Order of Restraint
> protects the table

Yard Sale

Unshaven, dirty overalls, hunched over, sitting in an old lawn chair, he watches as I roam his many garage sale tables, pick up a blender, check the price. "It works, she used it all the time", he grumbles. I nod, put it down.

Well used, but well maintained woodworking tools on the driveway – a table saw, electric drill press, planer, jig saw. Good prices. "They're still the best money can buy", he barks.

I look at an arm chair, notice the indentation in the seat cushion. Less harsh now, "She'd sit there, knit for hours, watch me work, talk about where we'd go." An old woman's clothing sways on hangers in a gentle breeze. Softly, "She was my best friend."

Stacks of old sail boat magazines cover a bench, marked FREE. I look at the pile, then at him. "Take as many as you want." he says. I reply with a question, "A passion for sailing I see. No longer interested?" He shrugs, smiles a half smile, points at well worn drawings for a sail boat…says, "No use anymore. It's finished."

> varnished teak,
> polished brass…
> traveling alone

Unsettling Settled

Dear Sir,

Thank you for your submissions. They were read with interest but do not meet the current needs of our publication. I invite and encourage you to submit material again in the future.

Sincerely,

Editor,

Why the rejection? What don't they like about my work? And why the formal salutation? Just a form letter?

Yah, I've heard this before – "It's not you, it's me". That sucks.

His head spins with imagined criticism, self-doubt. He wants to write back, "What do I have to re-write to make it acceptable?", "How do I improve – please tell me what I've got to do?", "Would it make a difference if I tried again – is your mind already made up?"

"Ah hell, do I really want to improve? Screw off. Who needs you anyway?"

> television blare
> a pen discarded
> on the writing pad

Retracted Invitation?

From a friend, a general invitation in my e-mail invites the many recipients on a hiking trip into a mountain area of meadows and high ridges. Having seen pictures of the spectacular views, I definitely want to get there.

However, I haven't hiked for many years. This trip starts with a 19 km hike crossing several thigh high streams, only to arrive at a piece of rocky ground on which to pitch a small tent and an all too thin air mattress. The trip will be supported by pack horses so I only have to carry a light day pack. Still, I have my trepidations. I send my friend some questions:

What is the maximum weight for the pack which will be carried in by horse?

Who supplies toilet paper?

Where will I plug in my CPAP breathing machine?

Do we assume we could be separated on the long walk in, and bring our own high powered rifle, or at least bear spray?

Who carries in the 30,000 btu heater to keep me warm at night?

Who brings the first aid kit, and will there be medicinal marijuana?

What television channels will we get at camp?

Who will bring out my carcass?

It's been days since I sent in my request and I haven't had a reply. The invitation said the hike was to start today.

> almost full moon
> the kid dressed
> for street hockey, not picked

Resilience

aftershock after shock
people pitch in
to help one another

She discovers food and water left in her entranceway. Old men show up at her doorstop to make sure she has what she needs. Living with a friend, they share supplies like water, food and a kerosene heater; sleep crowded together in one room; eat by candlelight; share stories.

Sleep is disturbed by more tremors. At night, the stars are bright above this now dark city without electricity. With no traffic, night sounds are clear.

earthquake relief
charity pours in
with the rain water

* the stimulus for this piece was an e-mail from an earthquake survivor named Anne that was circulating on the internet just after the earthquake in Japan.

Such a Fool

The offer appeals to me. All I have to do is go online and give some contact information and I'm entered into their contest. Seems easy enough.

I fill out the form but find a glitch when trying to fill in the date field. It's not clear what date is being requested – today's or my birthday. Everything I enter is rejected. I give up, hit the submit button.

The form just bounces back at me with deleted fields and red circles around EXCLAMATION points both for those troublesome date fields, and some fields that had been completed properly.

Insanely, I try to do it again. EXCLAMATION points.

I want a chance to win this damn prize so I look on the website for a 'Contact Us'. One hasn't been provided. Was this an intended frustration on their part, or the mistake of some web designer deep in their organization?

> the robin tugs
> at the resisting worm
> first day of April

Saturdays

a full day planned
an early rush
to get the newspaper

Sitting in front of a computer, she works on her crossword puzzle –
periodically looking up the clues on the internet, spell checking
with her online dictionary. She does this for hours.

When she has completed as much as she can, she calls her sister
who's been doing the same. They talk excitedly about the clues
they figured out, share the answers they have that the other didn't
get, express frustration for those that are obscure. Invariably they
admit to guessing a few words, and suspect they guessed wrong.
Finally, the newspaper sheet is set aside.

empty squares
the chores
go undone

Springtime Thinking

Sitting at the table, dinner done, dishes clean, she asks to talk.

"I want to have another baby."

"Not me, I can barely manage with the one we have."

"When we were dating, we talked about four or five."

"Then, I didn't know how hard it would be." *And back then, I'd say anything to get into your pants.*

"We need to talk about this."

"I don't know why. I just can't."

"Well you better think about that some more!"

She storms off, slams the bedroom door and I hear the lock click shut.

This morning, stiff and sore after a night of sleeping on a too short couch, I sit at the table. Shaking hands hold a cup. I watch the ripples in the coffee. I think about how one thing leads to another.

I hear the door open. She comes down the hall.

Eye contact. My slow nod of acquiescence. Her smile.

> snow melt
> the purple flower
> of the first crocus

Belly Laughs

> parked sled
> walking the halls
> of the hospital

I enter what appears to be an abandoned part of the hospital. This is where I'm supposed to be for a cardiopulmonary exercise test. My confusion arrests. Someone comes from a hidden office area to collect me. A smile appears on his face as he realizes who I am. "Remember me?", he asks.

> childish enthusiasm
> wish lists
> arrived in the mail

Black knee high boots tucked in a corner. White trimmed red coat and white shirt suspended on a coat hanger, I'm shirtless, wires attached to my chest, back and shoulders. A blood pressure cuff bands my upper arm. A breathing tube clenched in my teeth pokes through a heavy beard. My feet are strapped into harnesses on the pedals of the stationary bike. I'm given instructions to pedal at a steady speed and to listen for periodic directions to inhale quickly and deeply.

In preparation for my big day, I'm here to assess my state of health – my ability to work long hours and to lift heavy bags. I pedal steady. The tension on the pedals increases at one minute intervals.

> northern nights
> in the update,
> production is on schedule

Every few minutes, I'm asked to point to a chart to show how much discomfort I feel – in my breathing, in my legs. At the beginning, I point at the lowest rating of 0. Then 1. More work, then 2.

After seven minutes my breathing discomfort is at 8, the pain in my legs is growing and I'm at 6. My customary chuckles are abated as the rhythm of my puffing matches that of the rise and fall of the pedals.

> waist buttons pop
> from the strain
> fresh snow

The observing doctor says, "Only a little longer", a concerned expression on his face. He watches my heart rate rise to the recommended maximum. It's clear that he doesn't want to be the cause of my last breath. As I near collapse, he ends the test and helps me off the bike.

The doctor summarizes what he has observed. Nods to my rotund belly, gently suggests that my breathing may be constrained mechanically, places undue stress on my heart. 'You have to do something. You can't keep this up."

> long ride north
> twenty to thirty minutes
> of exercise prescribed

Telephone Tag

This is Jones. I'm out on a project. Leave a message. Beep...

"Boss, This is Ralph. I won't be in to work today as I've had an accident."

Hey, It's Ralph. Can't come to the phone right now so leave a message. Go Giants! Beep...

"Ralph, you have to tell me more than that. What happened?"

This is Jones. I'm out on a project. Leave a message. Beep...

"Sorry I couldn't get to the phone in time to answer. It's awkward to tell you Boss. After work yesterday, a bunch of my bodies and I went to the bar. They like to unwind on Saturday nights, and I like to join them, even though I work the next day. You know how it is – you just need to spend time with your friends. I try to keep to just a six pack so I'm not hung over the next morning, but sometimes I lose count."

Hey, It's Ralph. Can't come to the phone right now so leave a message. Go Giants! Beep...

"Ralph. What the hell is going on? Do you just have a hangover and sleep in? What about the accident?"

This is Jones. I'm out on a project. Leave a message. Beep...

"No that's not it Boss. I did sleep in again, but I woke dazed, startled at the time, and rushed to put my pants on. I put my leg in my pants, straightened up and banged my head on the television set that hangs on the wall by the foot of my bed. I lost my balance, collapsed, hit my knee on the heater, wrenched away in agony, and sprained my ankle as I crashed into my lamp. Butter helped the burn but I can't put any weight on my ankle."

200

Hey, It's Ralph. Can't come to the phone right now so leave a message. Go Giants! Beep...

"So... have you seen a Doctor? When does he think you can come back to work?"

This is Jones. I'm out on a project. Leave a message. Beep...

"Well Boss, I don't think I need a Doc. Right now, I've placed my foot in a sort of a noose, run the rope to the doorknob and I'm pulling on the rope to keep the ankle under traction. A huge bag of ice is draped over the ankle to reduce the inflammation so I think I'll be able to come in tomorrow. I won't let you down."

Hey, It's Ralph. Can't come to the phone right now so leave a message. Go Giants! Beep...

"Ralph. It's Jones. Thanks for letting me know. Don't worry about coming in tomorrow. Take as long as you need to get that ankle to heal. Right now, project funding has been cut back a little and we have to cut back on manpower. I'll let you know when we need you."

Superbowl Sunday
winners
and losers

Christmas Carol

Three and a half years old, articulate for her age, confident, a defined purpose in mind, sitting on Santa's lap, comfortable with this stranger.

"What would you like for Christmas?" his rote question.

"A mommy and daddy" she declares.

Taken aback, he asks "What happened to your Mom and Dad?"

"I never had a Daddy. Mommy made me on her own. She says I'm special that way."

"But you said you want a new Mommy?"

Dipping her head just a little, and with a tear drop forming in her eye, she said "Granpa said she was called away… won't be coming back."

Santa pauses, unsure what to say, no longer bored by the repetition of his day.

"Granpa says I need to get a new mommy and maybe I could get a daddy too. He can't take care of me any more. He's going away soon too."

A froggy croak erupts from Santa's mouth, he catches his breath and asks, "What kind of Mommy and Daddy would you like?"

"Someone who's lonely, needs to have someone special around to love them."

"You have a lot of love to give?"

"Oh Yes. I love everybody."

> Christmas wishes
> a puppy
> under the tree

An Untold Story

A frayed rope holds a fishing boat to the dock. Peeling paint, wood trim bleached from the sun, stacks of torn nets, no one aboard; no one present on the dock.

And then, she saunters along the quay. Blond dreadlocks, flip-flops, cut-offs, halter top and deeply tanned skin. She nods, makes eye contact, steps up to the deck and asks, "Want to come aboard for a toke?"

> thinning fog
> a lady bug
> lights on my sleeve

Moth to the Light*

Late at night, thoughts in turmoil, I pass from an unlit street, into the light cast through the windows of a downtown diner.

Inside, they sit, side by side, coffee mugs and elbows on the counter, her studying her nails, him staring forward. They're together, but seem as isolated as I feel.

Another man, his back to me, steam rising from a fresh cup of coffee, keeps to himself. How can he keep his eyes off her?

It looks warm inside, a step toward the door, a chance to see her, even though she's with him... maybe she's realized that he's not that great after all...

... but I pass on by, a solo nighthawk – it's less painful that way.

> that stunning red dress
> her "Dear John" letter
> in my pocket

* This ekphrastic piece was stimulated by an Edward Hopper painting of a downtown diner titled *Nighthawks*, completed in 1942.

A Shift in Sexual Demographics

She reads out loud, "87% of respondents admitted to being non-monogamous." We both know she's one of the 13%. Today she says, "I'm tired of being a minority."

> the panther's dark stare
> bowels churn
> and his gut burns

Free Verse Haibun

Periodically, I'm moved to write a piece in free verse. This is my experiment – a free verse poem followed by a three line haiku. Perhaps these are not legitimately haibun, but as they include prose followed by a haiku, I include them here for your consideration. Possibly neither free verse poetry or haibun, they are just another way to share some intimate moments.

Dissolving Time

chewing
on slowly passing minutes
wandering thoughts
fill my day
like grey trees
fill a winter forest

no specific thing
grabs attention
nor compels an action
so I shuffle papers,
worry the beads,
fill spaces with lethargy
in otherwise
meaningless moments

self-inflicted,
these entrapments
spend the time
I can't afford to spend

in an interview before
inoperable cancer took
Warren Zevon's music away,
he gave this advice…
"Enjoy every sandwich"
I wonder what it will take
for me to find the conviction
to eat so well.

                    new romance
                    a breakfast
                    of delicacies

A Smile Not a Smile

an infant, aged one,
on the floor, on his butt
dressed in fineries,
booted feet splayed apart,
tugs on a shoe lace,
looks at the camera

eyes wide open, a smile
all the elements just right
for the portrait that pleases
the camera man, and his mother

sixty years later he looks
at that picture, and sees
the boy within, recognizes
the smile that isn't a smile
the eyes wide open,
but not the eyes of delight

he sees the underlying
apprehension, suspended breath,
the persistent question
– "what do they want from me?"

his answer
two children,
two grandchildren

Can't Wait Anymore

suspended, waiting
for a motor part
to arrive
so I can take
an important journey.

feels like life
- I have to go
but not sure where
or when.

urgency drives me
to get there
before she delivers
her new baby,
to be there for her
as I should be.

impatience urges me
to get there,
somewhere, anywhere
before I die.

the fragile life
of a new baby
hangs by a cord
waiting for
the right moment.

the ragged life
of an old man
rushes toward
the last.

a new outlook
the smell of dirty diapers
and her delighted laugh

A Life Force?

If there is a life force
that inhabits and energizes
all living things, do flowering plants
feel their aging as their petals
fade, turn brown, drop to the ground,
becoming worm food and nothing more?
Do their egos fail as decline
brings lowered yields of flowering buds,
as wondrous colours subside,
and the ability to excite the air
dissipates into withering scent?

Does the once flowered tree
experience an intense loneliness
as it grows invisible, draws fewer
and fewer bees to its side?
In despair, does it take note as
a once personal beauty is
replaced by the every day colour
of branches that no longer bear fruit?

Do adult birds weep in anticipation
as their offspring fledge, practice flight
and ultimately leave the nest?
In the wilderness, to what extent
does each parent think that life's purpose
is over as the den empties of life
leaving a litter of bones and dung?
Do accumulated territories matter
once one is no longer able to
walk their full breadth, or to defend them?

Silently blessed by the presence
of the universe, by an electricity
that fires cells, moves body fluid,
gives purpose to each action, silently,
attached, to each of us, a life cycle,
a story that becomes our own.

Do we each feel the slow ebbing
of that spirit as we are drawn
to a too premature closing,
to the mingling of our remains
in the dirt and ashes of time?

> the tightly woven brown
> turns to white fluff
> snow on bulrushes

Spirit Mending

Like a bicycle inner tube
nailed to an old barn door,
my spirit bakes each day,
in the hot sun, and
freezes each night
in cold realization
of failed results
and meager outcomes.
Infinitesimal or huge
– failures all the same.

Shriveled, taught,
elasticity lost, this inner self
hangs from a rusted nail.

Each day, as I awake
to new hope, my spirit
breathes a simple air,
stretches through
yesterday's dull aches
and coloured bruises.

On a healing journey, I walk
forest paths, climb rocky points,
scuff pebbles on the beach.

Afresh, I notice flowers,
detect their scent,
hear bird calls
get their answering reply.
I watch insects dart,
buzz and disappear;
smell composting leaves,
taste the tart and sweet
of blackberries from
blood red vines.

Today is better
than yesterday
and the day before.
I go to bed silently
chanting a new mantra –
"I'm retired now. I – me
choose what I want to do,
how I measure myself!"
My breathing sets the
rhythm by which I review
the results of the day.
I lazily descend into sleep
as a sigh emerges from my soul.

Only to wake again to the
feel of the rusted nail,
and the sad constrictions
of failures past.

> the morning of a new year
> this year's calendar
> similar to the last

The Pier Of Life

A boy stands on the pier of life,
watches others sail to new lands,
knowing his turn must come.

He wonders how to be a man,
takes on his responsibilities
with reluctance and uncertainty
filching the easy way till it ain't easy anymore

He makes his choices
believing he knows what he is doing,
while understanding that he doesn't have a clue

When insecurity declares
that he isn't man enough to travel on his own
he pretends his love and finds
a partner for the journey

In the new land, with little wealth to his name,
he uses his wits and joy in his heart
to create what he can and steal what he can't.

He takes his place – with bluster, bravado
and an arrogant claim that he can read the stars -
to hide the feelings of a lost little boy
in this strange new world

Like all imperialists before him,
he eagerly stakes his claim to native territory,
pillaging where he can, investing his labours where he must

Clumsily, he assaults this strange landscape,
imposes his comforts and traditions,
ignores the wisdom of those that came before,
calls them ignorant savages that must be civilized

His wealth emerges, his larder fills, his family grows,
his time passes – and his heart empties,
missing the lost thrills of ignorance and youth

His work diminishes, time slows,
leaving reflections on what has been,
what could have been, what has yet to be
in this journey he has fumbled through

A man stands on the pier of life,
watches others sail to new lands,
knowing his turn must come.

> dew this sunny morning
> a shroud picked out
> to cover his coffin

Edward Hopper's Night Man*

God! Another dark hour attending to the lonely.
I know it's my job as an angel of the night
to pull them into the light, give them hope,
and serve their lost souls… but really?

They just sit there, blind to the riches
before them, unable to breath in the joy
that comes from a good women, unable to smell
the deep satisfactions of a plain Americano,
wrapped up in their suits and fedoras, toking
carelessly on their burnt-out cigarettes.
Immobile in their solitude, they hunch over,
elbows on the counter, watching steam rise,
thinking about what they don't have,
losing sight of what's before them,
contemplating their empty lives
and wondering if its time to pull the trigger.

Ignoring me, of course, not seeing the sprite that I am,
a rescuer of men who've fallen overboard.
I throw them a simple line, with my best intentions -
"Hey mister. Another coffee, a donut,
or are you ready for bacon and eggs,
pancakes hot off the griddle?"
I see them all, but they don't see me.
Drawn in by warm light and deep oak,
they sit in a pool of goodwill, slowly fill
the hole in themselves. God that feels good.

> a coffee shop at night
> the counter boy gathers
> up the left overs

* A somewhat ekphrastic piece based on Edward Hopper's painting
  titled *Nighthawks*, oil on canvas, 1942.

Negistentialism

I have a bleak sense
of what life is about -
eat, shit, procreate,
die, become worm food,
some level of engagement
in relationship I suppose

it's a human condition
to find a deeper meaning
or purpose to one's existence
but I have no religious
or spiritual questions -
just the premise
that we are all parasites
ultimately destroying this planet,
essentially alone, misunderstood,
appreciated less by others
than one appreciates oneself

I have no personal desire
to 'grow and develop'
as a more complete human being
I gave up on that pursuit
a long time ago

I just want to be present
and share what seems sharable
when we get together,
to be respectful and compassionate
in response to what is shared with me.

            companionship
            the sun shines and wind
            moves the clouds

Deathbed Regrets?

so what might I regret
as the last breath departs?

failing to make my fortune
and gather my fame?
loving too little
while loving too much?
unwritten books
and long dead projects?
provincial travels
and the world unseen?
friendships abandoned
and opportunities lost?
the lives of children
unwatched, unnoticed?

will death's rattle
be the only sound
in an empty room?

> the hiker kicks
> a rotting log
> a beetle scurries from the light

Closing

Through reading my haibun, you've had a chance to get to know something about me, and hopefully through self-reflection, something more about yourself. I've worked to be as open as possible in my writing, and to share with you what is real for me.

However, there is a fiction to all of this in that memories are distorted, attention to specific moments is never complete, and the process of denial keeps things below conscious awareness. I am not completely this person described in these writings but I am present in each.

Remembering Life

I wish I remembered 'life', but I don't. Not really.

So much of my life has been sublimated beyond easy recall. Along with the simple loss of memory attributed to growing old, my circuits were disrupted the many times I changed my places of residence, dramatically changed careers, changed intimate partners. I no longer remember which life I lived – possibly someone else's.

I married young out of a pregnant necessity, moved through that life in a state of dissociation and shock as I tried to cope with the many responsibilities I hadn't anticipated. Feeling the anxious need to provide for family, I buried myself in work, changed environments as I changed careers, stayed long enough to feel important in each place, but short enough to discover that I really wasn't. The memories of each of those lives disappeared with the adjustments I made to survive in the new.

This isn't to say that I don't have any memories. Although infrequent and fleeting, I do recall moments as a child, adolescent, young adult, workaholic, and then old man – but I don't trust that such recall represents what really happened.

> a detailed weather forecast
> that didn't come true
> windblown clouds

Secret Satisfactions

I've been told I embarrass myself by writing so openly about my moments of despondency, my failures to accomplish my goals, my weaknesses of character. I think not, but then I am not the judge of such things. However, this comment reminds me that I do not focus enough on the good things in my life.

I seldom write about the satisfactions I feel within my family relationships, pride that I have in the accomplishments of others that are important to me, joy in the doing of those things that bring me into the moment, delight in watching others around me make their own discoveries.

All of this feels too normal, has no angst and generates no compulsion to work something out through writing. The things that I accomplish seldom feel like more than what I should achieve.

Consequently, the 'me' that I show has his pants down, holds his head low. The public 'me' has sagging shoulders, a pinched face, self-disappointment in his eyes. The 'me' I show appears smaller than he is.

> quiet dinner
> a school report card
> left in his room

Acknowledgements

My introduction to the writing of haibun came from Dr. Ray Rasmussen, author of *Landmarks: A Haibun Collection.* He generously shared his enthusiasm and knowledge about haibun and haiku and showed me something of how to write in this format through examples from his own writing and articles and commentaries he authored about haibun. He provided one-to-one critique of my early work, then formed the on-line Haibun Writer's Workgroup with Lynn Edge, and then later the on-line Haibun Study Group. He invited me into both. I am very grateful for this wise and enthusiastic influence.

In both of these forums, I had the opportunity to participate with others who were also learning to write haibun more effectively. I acknowledge the many folks who participated in these workgroups, reading and critiquing my contributions and those of others. I very much gained from what they shared of themselves in their work, and the feedback they gave in reaction to mine. Many of the haibun in this book arrived at their current form because of the suggestions members of these groups provided. Thank you all.

Several editors saw fit to publish a few of my pieces. I give thanks to the folks at Haibun Today, Contemporary Haibun and Contemporary Haibun Online, and Simply Haiku.

Thank you to Katherine Caine who read and provided feedback on this collection of haibun, and to Dianne Tuterra who read, provided feedback and helped with the organization of the haibun into the different categories. Another thank you to Ray Rasmussen who laboriously found many typos in the previous version of this document.

About The Author

Gary R. Ford, MBA, PhD

After achieving undergraduate and master's degrees in business administration plus a PhD in Educational Psychology, Gary has had a varied career. He worked as a lecturer in the business administration program at the University of Alberta. He practiced as a registered psychologist providing counseling to individuals, couples, and families, as well as doing organizational development work with health, social service, legal and educational institutions.

Seeking practical experience, he then made a radical career choice and operated a retail and corporate sales organization for 20 years, after which he entered his first retirement. Unable to sit still for long, he then worked as a Dean of Business with a start-up Canadian university for five years. He retired again during a period surrounding the illness and subsequent death of his wife.

In this second retirement, Gary has been writing a series of books on sales, problem solving, and peer counseling based on the insight process of Getting The S.P.I.C.E^3. In between these projects, he engaged in creative writing in the haibun genre.

Gary is currently spending his time engaged in writing and amateur photography. You can see his work at www.garyrford.ca.

Publishing Credits

Gopher Holes – previously published in *Contemporary Haibun* Vol 6 and *Contemporary Haibun On-line* June 2005 1:1

A Polished Stone – published in *Contemporary Haibun Online*, December 2005, 1:3

Lingering – previously published in *Haibun Today*, 7:3, September 2013

What Legacy? – previously published in *Simply Haiku*, November-December 2004

Crossing Paths – previously published in *Simply Haiku* Nov/Dec 2004

Just A Moment – previously published in *Haibun Today*, 7:4, December 2013

Untold Stories – previously published in *Haibun Today*, 7:4, December 2013

INSIGHT
PUBLISHERS

Box 2 Site 3 RR #1 South
Thorsby, Alberta, Canada
T0C 2P0
www.garyrford.ca/insight